CUBE
BOOK

CUBE
BOOK

HORSES

WHITE STAR PUBLISHERS

EDITED BY

VALERIA MANFERTO DE FABIANIS

texts by
GABRIELE BOISELLE
HENRY DALLAL
ATTILA KORBELY
PAOLO MANILI
SENIO SENSI
MEDFORD TAYLOR

graphic design
CLARA ZANOTTI

graphic layout
MARIA CUCCHI

editorial staff
GIADA FRANCIA
ENRICO LAVAGNO
ALBERTO BERTOLAZZI

translation
TIMOTHY STROUD

© 2005 WHITE STAR S.P.A.
VIA CANDIDO SASSONE, 22-24
13100 VERCELLI - ITALY
WWW.WHITESTAR.IT

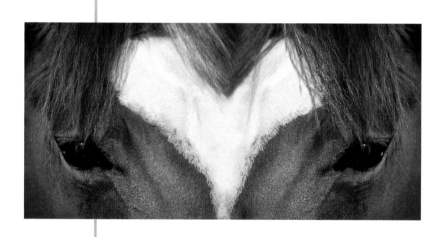

ISBN 13: 978-88-544-0051-1

REPRINTS:
3 4 5 6 11 10 09 08 07

Printed in Singapore
Color separation: Chiaroscuro, Turin

CONTENTS

HORSES

1 ● Great Britain. The graceful profile of an Arabian.

2-3 ● France. The semi-wild horses of the Camargue.

4-5 ● USA. A herd of horses in the Southwest.

6-7 ● Italy. Pure competition at the Palio in Siena!

9 ● USA. This bay is distinguished by the white heart standing out on its forehead.

11 ● The Netherlands. Friesians boast proud and wavy manes

12-13 ● USA. An Appaloosa with a leopard coat.

14-15 ● Austria. A Haflinger pony galloping.

16-17 ● Argentina. A *gaucho* and Criollos on the pampa.

Introduction

by Paolo Manili

OVER THE MILLENNIA THE HORSE HAS EXERCISED AN IMMENSE INFLUENCE OVER THE DEVELOPMENT OF HUMANITY; CIVILIZATION WOULD HAVE EVOLVED DIFFERENTLY HAD THE CREATURE NOT EXISTED. IT WAS IN EARLIEST PREHISTORY THAT MAN TRANSFORMED THE HORSE FROM A TASTY PREY INTO A MEANS OF TRANSPORT, WORKING TOOL AND WAR MACHINE. IN ADDITION, BY AROUSING PASSIONS AND AMBITION IN MAN, THE HORSE GAVE RISE TO GREAT DEEDS, ENCOURAGED HUMAN MIGRATIONS AND CONQUESTS, AND DETERMINED HUMAN EVENTS AND DESTINIES. THE HORSE HAS ALSO INSPIRED COUNTLESS GENERATIONS OF PAINTERS AND SCULPTORS, POETS AND MUSICIANS, WHOSE REPRESENTATIONS OF THE HORSE'S

● Iceland. A wavy mane frames the gentle gaze of an Iceland pony, a docile, affectionate and reliable animal.

BREEDS and their
CHARACTERISTICS

GABRIELE BOISELLE

- France. A splendid Arabian sorrel.

SOME BREEDS JUST TUG AT ONE'S HEART, BUT ABOVE ALL OTHERS THE ARABIANS DO. CHARMING, BEAUTIFUL, INTELLIGENT AND PLAYFUL, THEY ARE EAGER TO CONNECT WITH PEOPLE; THEY ARE CURIOUS ABOUT EVERYTHING NEW AND TRY TO PLEASE THEIR HUMANS, WHOM THEY BELIEVE TO BE THEIR OWN. THEN THERE ARE FRIESIAN HORSES, ABSOLUTELY GENTLE AND HUMBLE WITH THOSE WHO WORK WITH THEM DAY BY DAY. BUT THE MOMENT THEY ARE FREE, THEY FLY OVER THE EARTH, NO LONGER EARTHBOUND, WITH THEIR FLOATING MANES AND 'FEATHERS' AROUND THEIR LEGS AND THEIR HUGE TAILS WHICH SEEM TO BE CREATED OF WAVES OF BLACK HAIR. THEY

Portugal. A white Lusitanian plays in Mediterranean waves.

INTRODUCTION Breeds and their Characteristics

WERE BRED TO IMPRESS IN FRONT OF THE SPECIAL FRIESIAN SJEEß WITH THEIR EXTENDED TROT. BUT WHILE THEY ARE GREAT DRESSAGE HORSES THEY ARE ALSO IDEAL FOR CIRCUS WORK. NO HORSE SHOW CAN EXPECT TO SUCCEED WITHOUT THE PERFORMANCE OF FRIESIAN HORSES. THEIR CLOSE RELATIVES, THE ANDALUSIANS, WHICH ARE MOSTLY GREY HORSES WITH FLOATING MANES, CAN BE ADMIRED AS WELL IN THE DIFFERENT DISCIPLINE OF HIGH-STYLE DRESSAGE. CENTURIES AGO THEY WERE BRED TO PERFORM THE CAPRIOLE AND PESADE AS USEFUL FIGHTING STRATE-GIES IN BATTLE. LATER ON, HORSEMANSHIP BECAME AN ART AND TODAY THE LIPIZZANER HORSES PERFORM THESE FIGURES IN THE SPANISH RIDING SCHOOL IN VIEN-

INTRODUCTION

NA. ALL OVER EUROPE THERE ARE DIFFERENT BREEDS OF HORSES DESCENDED FROM FOREBEARS BRED FOR SPECIAL MILITARY NEEDS: CAVALRY HORSES FOR WAR; HORSES EASY TO RIDE; AND FAST HORSES ABLE TO JUMP OVER OBSTACLE. THEN THERE ARE THE WORKING HORSES; HEAVY BREEDS FOR PULLING WAGONS, TRANSPORTING GOODS, AND FOR PLOWING FIELDS. ON SUCH HORSES' SHOULDERS LAYING THE RESPONSIBILITY FOR AGRICULTURAL LIFE. IN THEIR MILLIONS THEY BROUGHT IN THE HARVEST AND ASSURED WEALTH AND PROSPERITY. SADLY, WITH THE ADOPTION OF INDUSTRIAL MACHINERY MOST OF THEM WERE NO LONGER NEEDED AND WERE SLAUGHTERED. ONLY A DECADE AGO DID PEOPLE BEGIN TO UNDERSTAND

INTRODUCTION Breeds and their Characteristics

THAT THEY HAD TO PRESERVE THESE OLD BREEDS IN RECOGNITION OF ALL THE WORK THEIR ANCESTORS HAD DONE. AS A RESULT, THERE IS NOW A RENAISSANCE IN THE BREEDING OF DRAFT HORSES IN EUROPE AND AMERICA. OLD BREEDS LIKE THE ARDENNER, PERCHERON, NORIKER, BRETONE, COB NORMAND, SHIREHORSE, CLYDESDALES AND OTHERS ARE BECOMING KNOWN AGAIN, HORSE LOVERS VERY OFTEN UNDERESTIMATE THE VALUE OF PONY BREEDS. THEY ARE SEEN AS KIDS' HORSES, NOT TO BE TAKEN SERIOUSLY. BUT NOW, WHEN THE PRICE OF A 'SPORT' PONY CAN EASILY BE TRIPLE THE PRICE OF A REASONABLY ACCOMPLISHED SHOW HORSE, PEOPLE ARE HAVE BECOME AWARE OF THE POTENTIAL VALUE OF

INTRODUCTION Breeds and their Characteristics

THE "SMALL ONES." IN FACT, OVER HISTORY, PONIES HAVE BEEN USED IN AGRICULTURAL WORK AND IN PULLING WAGONS, JUST LIKE DRAUGHT HORSES. FOR EXAMPLE, IN NORWAY, THE FJORD PONY FROM WAS USED ON THE VERY STEEP HILLS ALONG THE FJORDS, WHERE BIGGER HORSES HAD TOO LITTLE ROOM TO WORK SUCCESSFULLY. IN IRELAND, THE CONNEMARA PONY WAS ONCE A REAL WORKING BREED THAT PULLED CARTS. ONLY ON THE WEEKENDS DID THE FARMERS RACE THEM AGAINST EACH OTHER. TODAY THE CONNEMARAS PRODUCE SUPERCLASS JUMPING PONIES FOR INTERNATIONAL COMPETITIONS. FOR CEN-TURIES EVERY COUNTRY BRED THE HORSES IT NEED-ED. THE BLOODLINES OF MOST BREEDS HAVE BEEN IM-

Breeds and their Characteristics
Introduction

PROVED BY ENGLISH THOROUGHBREDS AND BY ARA-BIANS. BUT THE ACTUAL DIVERSITY OF THE BREEDS RESULTS FROM THE SELECTIVE BREEDING DIFFERENT BREEDERS HAVE UNDERTAKEN. IN THE FUTURE, WE WILL HAVE DEMANDS FOR HIGH-QUALITY STOCK, AND HIGH-INTENSITY DEMANDS AND PEOPLE WILL ALSO BREED THE HORSE MOST SUITABLE FOR COMPETITION AND FOR RECREATIONAL RIDING, EITHER BASED ON THE WESTERN OR ON THE ENGLISH RIDING SYSTEM. AND FINALLY, THERE IS ONE VERY IMPORTANT REASON TO BREED HORSES, NOW THAT WE NO LONGER NEED THEM TO ENSURE OUR DAILY SURVIVAL – THE LOVE WE FEEL FOR THEM IN GETTING TO KNOW THEM.

Iceland. Rustic and tough, the Iceland has a thick mane.

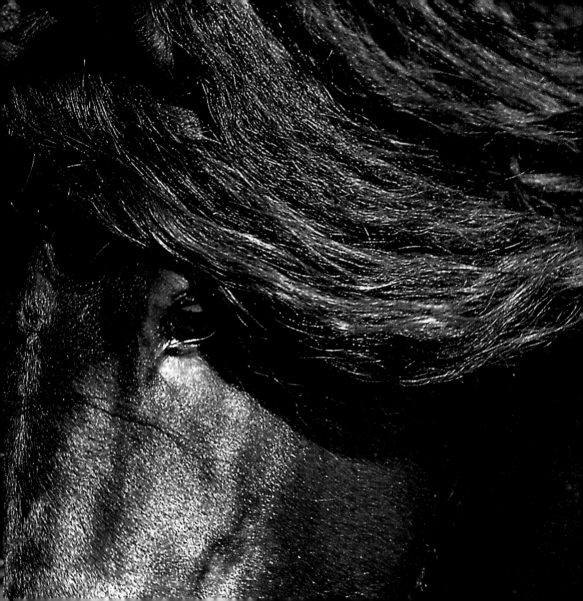

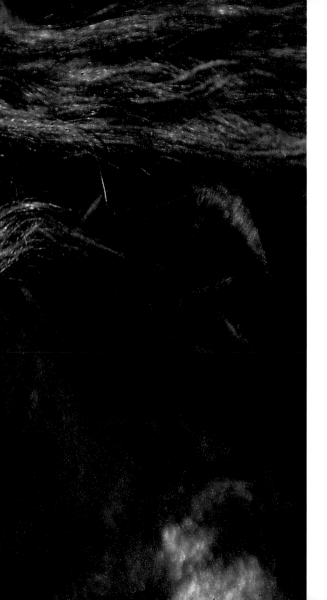

The Netherlands. Detail of a Friesian's raven-black, finely curled mane.

42 • The Netherlands. The Friesian's legs are not very long and the hocks are rather hairy.

43 • The Netherlands. A black Friesian plays in the rain.

The Netherlands. With their "curly" manes, Friesian horses boast unique elegance.

● The Netherlands.
Friesian at the gallop in the
Dutch countryside.

48 ● The Netherlands. Docile and intelligent, Andalusians are excellent dressage horses.

49 ● The Netherlands. A bridled Andalusian during a horse show.

Portugal. The docile and brave Lusitano is a very rare horse. It is estimated that there are only 20,000 or so around the world.

◆ Germany. The coats of Arabian horses vary in color, often with white splotches on the legs and head.

54 • Germany. Excellent riding horses, Arabians are quite frisky.

55 • Germany. A fine Arabian thoroughbred seems to pose proudly for the camera.

56 ● USA. Among Arabian horses, black ones with white hocks are the rarest and most sought after.

57 ● USA. Arabians are slender in build and of a nervous disposition.

58-59 ● Spain. Traditionally used for riding, Arabians seem born to gallop.

60 and 61 ● France. The sturdy head of a Comtois reveals its docile but willing nature.

62-63 ● France. The Comtois, a French draught horse, in the Middle Ages they were used as warhorses.

Iceland. The Iceland pony can ridden, but it can serve as a packhorse or draft animal. Moreover, it does not need to be stabled during the winter.

66 • Iceland. With its intelligent eye and fringed mane, Iceland ponies win sympathy at first glance.

66-67 • Iceland. The Iceland breed was created at the start of the 20th century by crossing local ponies with ponies that Norwegians brought to the islands.

Iceland. Seen here at the gallop in the snow, the Iceland is used as a saddle pony for inexpert riders.

● Great Britain. A long-established English breed from the Devon moors, the Dartmoor is strong and tireless.

Great Bretain. Though sturdy and unflagging, the long blond manes
of Shetland ponies make them seem cuddly.

Great Britain. Shetland ponies, originally from the Scottish mainland, in particular from the Orkneys and Isle of Shetland, were originally used as draught animals in mines and agriculture.

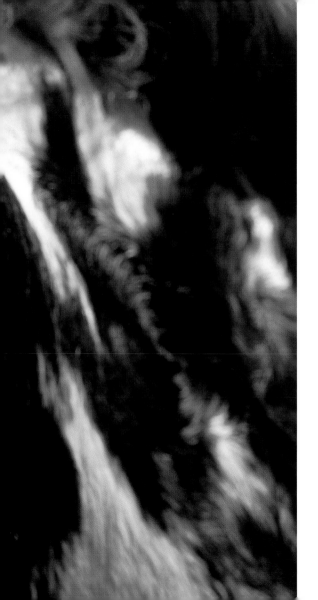

76-77 • Argentina. This close-up of a Criollo shows its tenacious and willing spirit.

77 and 78-79 • Argentina. A saddle horse, the Criollo was derived from crossing Arabian, Berber and Andalusian horses brought to South America by the Spanish.

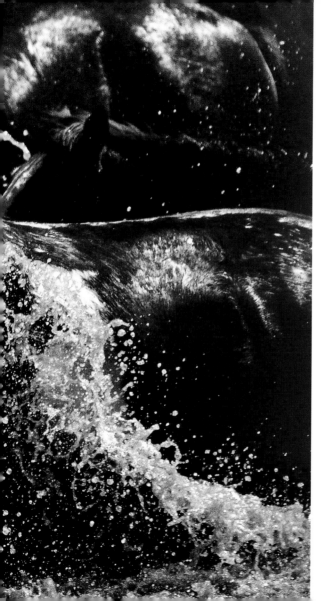

80-81 ● Argentina. The Criollo is the horse used by the *gauchos* of Latin America: they are sturdy, quick and agile in working with cattle.

82-83 ● Argentina. A Criollo's coat may be any of several shades, but is often marked with white and "mule lines."

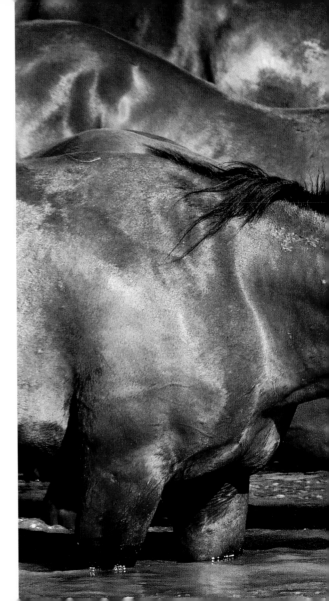

84-85 • Italy. Balanced and strong, and a good jumper, the Maremmano is generally bay.

86-87 • Italy. Originally short, strong and skittish, through crosses with English breeds the Maremmano has become the elegant and classic military horse of today.

● Ireland. The Gypsy Vanner is not really a breed but a horse of changeable appearance.

● Ireland. A saddle horse used by the military, and originally from Ireland, the Gipsy Vanner is currently used in equestrian tourism.

Ireland. The Gipsy Vanner is tough and dynamic: here we see their elegance, thick mane, long tail and hairy hocks.

Ireland. Bred with black, bay, gray and sorrel coats, Gipsy Vanners are also attractive piebald.

96-97 ● Austria. The Haflinger is originally from the Tyrol and therefore is strong and tough, fully suited to the alpine environment.

98-99 ● Austria. The Haflinger is considered a pony by experts due to its short, sturdy legs.

100 and 101 • Austria. This tyrolean pony's gentle expression belies a good
and intelligent nature.

102-103 • Austria. With their hooves hidden in the fresh snow, this Haflingers seems
perfectly at home on the mountain slopes.

104-105 and 105 ● Austria. A herd of Haflingers rises to a gallop on a snowy meadow in the Tyrol.

106-107 ● USA. The Pinto was first bred by Native Americans looking for "colored" wild horses to cross with horses of Spanish origin.

108 ● USA. The Pinto Arab's graceful action, especially at the gallop, is the breed's
most sought-after characteristic.

109 ● USA. This Pinto Arab filly displays all the typical gracefulness and elegance of her breed.

● USA. The Comanches were the first to begin selection of the Pinto, and ended up with the piebald we know.

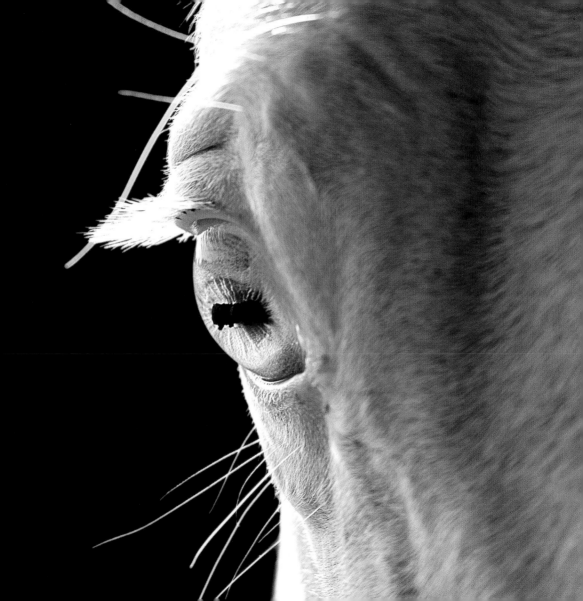

> " A LINEAGE AS NUMEROUS AND NOBLE AS THAT OF THE HORSE NATURALLY BOASTS GREAT "FAMILIES." THESE FAMILIES, COMMONLY KNOWN AS BREEDS, HAVE BEEN SHAPED BY MAN THROUGH THOUSANDS OF YEARS OF PATIENT WORK, AND HAVE CREATED THE MOST FORMIDABLE ALLIANCE EVER FORGED IN NATURE BETWEEN SUCH DIVERSE BEINGS. "

USA. Tough and characteristic in appearance, the Pinto has always been used to work with herds and in rodeos.

114 ● Germany. Manes flying in the wind, three Irish Tinkers break into a gallop.

115 ● Germany. The magnificent Irish Tinker is descended from horses selected by nomadic tinkers in Ireland.

Germany. Besides a dark complexion, Irish Tinker have spectacular long hair.

Germany. Because of its "square" structure, the Irish Tinker is an excellent workhorse, but it also has a docile and sensitive temperament.

120 ● USA. The Appaloosa is the classic "Western" horse, ideal for galloping, with plenty of speed and stamina. This type of coast is described as "marble."

121 ● USA. The Appaloosa's speckled coat gives this sturdy, vigorous and muscular horse a gentle complexion.

" A MONG HORSES, THE INFINITE COMBINATIONS OF COLORS AND PAT-
TERNS OF THEIR COATS REFLECT FAR MORE THAN MERE AESTHETIC SURFACE
TRAITS. THIS IS BECAUSE THEY IDENTIFY NOT ONLY A BREED OF HORSES BUT A
DISTINCT PERSONALITY. REGARDLESS OF WHETHER IT IS AN ARABIAN OR NOR-
MAN, FRIESIAN OR APPALOOSA, THE HORSE IS AN INDIVIDUAL FIRST AND FORE-
MOST, WITH ITS OWN PERSONALITY AMONG THE OTHERS. "

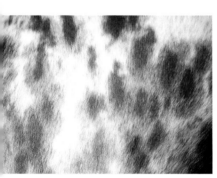 

122 and 123 • USA. The unique pattern on an Appaloosa's coat is a sort of identity
card that makes it immediately identifiable.

124-125 • Great Britain. Shire horses have distinctive long hair around their hocks.

126 ● Great Britain. Though taller, Shires resemble Friesians, a breed with which they were probably crossed in the Middle Ages.

127 ● Great Britain. Dark-haired Shire horses (whether black or bay) often have white patches.

128 ● USA. The Morgan horse, seen here with a palomino coat, is an excellent trotter.

129 ● USA. A horse from the American "frontier" like the Appaloosa, the Morgan is extremely versatile, and can be ridden or used as a draft animal. It is also ideal for competitions and parades.

● Great Britain. Two Shires at the gallop shine with sweat; note their huge and powerful muscles.

USA. Though particularly sensitive to sunlight, the American White is very vigorous and versatile. Muscular, with a broad chest and strong legs, American Whites have the characteristics of the breed's ancestor, Old King, who lived in the early 1900s.

134 ● Great Britain. The Thoroughbred is a graceful and nimble horse made for galloping.

135 ● Great Britain. An English Thoroughbred has an elegant, lean head.

HORSES in the WILD

ATTILA KORBELY

INTRODUCTION Horses in the Wild

THEIR 'WILDNESS' IS DEFINED BY ANOTHER IMPORTANT ASPECT. HUMANS USUALLY HERD HORSES WITH THE HELP OF A DOG OR A WHIP DOG, BUT A WILD HORSE CAN ONLY BE HERDED BY OTHER WILD HORSES. WHEN A STALLION WITH A HAREM APPROACHES ANOTHER, HE HERDS HIS MARES AND FOALS WITH NECK AND HEAD HELD STIFFLY AHEAD, EARS FLATTENED. BUT THESE CHARACTERISTI-CALLY STUBBORN ANIMALS DO NOT TEND TO LIKE THIS KIND OF DISPLAY, AND THE HERD TRIES TO KEEP THE IN-TRUDING STALLION AT BAY BY BITING AND KICKING. HOLD-ING TOGETHER A LARGE HAREM TAKES VIGILANCE, PER-SISTENCE AND ENERGY. ASIATIC WILD HORSES LIVE IN SO-CIAL GROUPS OR SOMETIMES SOLITARILY. UNLIKE DOMES-TICATED AND FERAL HORSES, THEY ARE EXTREMELY AG-

INTRODUCTION Horses in the Wild

GRESSIVE; A STALLION NOT ONLY PROTECTS ITS HAREM AND FOALS BUT SOMETIMES CONFRONTS OTHER HORSES FROM MILES AWAY TO FEND THEM OFF. THE WIND BRINGS A SHORT NEIGH ACROSS THE STEPPE. THE DOMINANT MALE LEAVES HIS HAREM AND CANTERS A FEW HUNDRED YARDS TOWARD THE SOURCE OF THE SOUND AND THEN STANDS STILL AND LISTENS WHILE FIXING HIS GAZE ON A SINGLE SPOT ON THE HORIZON. HIS HAREM GATHERS AROUND HIM, LOOKING WORRIED. IF NEITHER OF THE MALES BACKS OFF, THEN BOTH BEGIN FIERCELY TOSSING THEIR HEADS BACK AND FORTH, STAMPING ON THE GROUND WITH THEIR FRONT FEET, NEIGHING AND CALLING ON THE OTHER TO LEAVE. THEN, AS THOUGH THEY WERE PERFORMING AT A SPANISH RIDING SCHOOL,

Horses in the Wild

Introduction

THEY BEGIN A COLLECTED TROT TOWARD EACH OTHER ARCHING THEIR NECKS, EVENTUALLY JUMPING AT THE OTHER. THIS GESTURE IS JUST A SIMPLE SHOW OF POWER. WHEN THE STAKES ARE HIGHER, HOWEVER, AND A STALLION IS TRYING TO ACQUIRE A HAREM, THERE CAN BE BLOODSHED, SOMETIMES ENDING WITH THE DEATH OF ONE OF THE CONTENDERS. WILD HORSES HAVE A STRIKINGLY SWEET HABIT OF GROOMING: THEY STAND LANGUIDLY IN PAIRS, FACE TO FACE, FOR HOURS ON END, PECKING AND NIPPING AT EACH OTHER'S NECKS AND SIDES. DURING THIS "TEAM-BUILDING EXERCISE," AN AURA OF SERENITY DESCENDS OVER THE ANIMALS, MOMENTARILY OBSCURING THEIR WILD NATURE. . . .

145 ● France. A horse in the Camargue dashes across a ford in the Rhone delta.

146-147 ● France. The Rhone's chilly waters don't deter this playful herd.

France.
Since most of the herds
of horses of the
Camargue roam freely,
they must move often to
find food in the poor
lands of the marshes of
the Rhone Delta.

France. The horses of the Camargue, which are mainly gray in color, live semi-wild in the unique environment of the marshlands, to which they have adapted perfectly.

152 and 153 ● France. Camargue horses graze amid the corn poppies of the French Midi.

154-155 ● Portugal. Horses are free to gallop unimpeded on the plains of Portugal.

156-157 ● USA. North Americas open spaces seem ideal for wild horses.

Iceland. Originally selected as mountain horses, Iceland ponies are completely at ease on rough terrain and have no trouble climbing the steepest slopes.

Iceland. Ponies in Iceland have an extra gait known as *tølt*; it consists of bringing both legs on one side forward at the same time.

Iceland. The moors and grasslands on Iceland's hills are home to half-wild herds of horses.

Iceland. A line of ponies heads down a path in Iceland using the *tølt* gait.

166-167 ● Russia. Originally from Mongolia, Przewalsky horses are also known as wild Asian horses, though now they have almost disappeared from the Mongolian prairies.

168-169 ● Argentina. The permanently snow-covered Patagonian Andes provide an impressive backdrop for this cavalcade.

170-171 ● USA. A group of twenty or twenty-five mustangs at the gallop during a North American winter.

Great Britain. Born virtually immune to the cold, these ponies seem to enjoy themselves on the snowy slopes of Scotland.

USA. Elegant and fast,
Mustangs run free in the
American prairies.

176-177 ● USA. A ford in South Dakota provides a chance to cool down and play.

178-179 ● USA. Headed by a herd leader, these wild horses cross a swollen river in South Dakota.

180-181 ● USA. Impetuous natures and harmony of movement: a group of Thoroughbreds against the big sky of Montana.

182-183 ● USA. Wyoming's long grass country encourages these colts and fillies in their instinctive tendency to run.

The STEEDS of the FUTURE

SENIO SENSI

- France. This Arabian foal's sweet face shows the grace and beauty of this breed.

INTRODUCTION The Steeds of the Future

I HAVE ALWAYS THOUGHT THAT ANIMALS HAVE A SECRET LIFE THAT NOT EVEN ETHOLOGY CAN EXPLAIN. THEY HAVE A LIFE OF EMOTIONS, SENTIMENTS, SORROWS AND JOY PERHAPS EQUAL TO OUR OWN. THE INNERMOST SECRET LIES IN THE BIRTH OF AN ANIMAL: WHEREAS A WOMAN CAN EXPLAIN, ASK AND INFORM, UNLESS THEY LEAVE NATURE TO LOOK AFTER ITSELF, ANIMALS CAN ONLY LOOK AT US, ALMOST IMPLORINGLY, FOR SUPPORT. QUITE BY CHANCE, I WAS ONCE PRESENT AT THE BIRTH OF A FARM HORSE; NEEDING A BREECH DELIVERY, THE FOAL REQUIRED ALL THE EXPERIENCE, ENERGY AND DELICACY OF THE VET AND FARMER SO THAT IT WOULD NOT DIE DURING THE BIRTH. AS SOON AS THE PLACENTA DROPPED OUT

INTRODUCTION The Steeds of the Future

OF THE MOTHER'S BODY, SHE EXAMINED HER FOAL, AND SNIFFED AND LICKED IT. THE TINY NEWCOMER ATTEMPTED TO STAND UP BUT CLUMSILY FELL OVER. IT WAS MORE FORTUNATE A LITTLE LATER WHEN IT SEARCHED FOR ITS MOTHER'S TEAT AND BEGAN TO SUCK. GANGLING AND A LITTLE COMICAL, ITS LONG LEGS AND TINY BODY MADE IT RESEMBLE A BOY THAT HAD GROWN TOO QUICKLY. FOAL: THE OFFSPRING OF A HORSE. A TINY FOAL: THE DEFINITION OF TENDERNESS. FOALS SHOULD ALWAYS HAVE A CHILD CLOSE BY FOR RECIPROCAL BENEFIT: SO THAT THE CHILD WILL LEARN TO RESPECT ANIMALS AND THE FOAL WILL HAVE A LESS TRAUMATIC EXPERIENCE WHEN IT COMES TO BE TRAINED, AS, THOUGH THIS IS A STAN-

The Steeds of the Future

Introduction

DARD OCCURRENCE, IT IS AN UNNATURAL ONE. A FOAL IS THE SYMBOL OF JOYOUS FREEDOM. IT PLAYS IN ITS FIELD WITHOUT LOGIC OR RULES, THEN RETURNS TO ITS MOTHER TO LEARN AND IMITATE PROUDLY HER PHYSICAL MOVEMENTS. WATCHING A FOAL AND ITS MOTHER I SOMETIMES WONDER WHAT TYPE OF COMMUNICATION LINKS THE TWO OTHER THAN TEACHING BY EXAMPLE. TEACHING A YOUNGSTER HOW TO LIVE ITS LIFE IS DIFFICULT FOR ONE AND ALL, BUT MORE SO TO THOSE WHO ARE SUBJECTED TO THE DEMANDS OF MAN. PERHAPS THIS IS A SECRET THAT IT IS BETTER NOT TO FIND OUT.

France. An Arabian colt explores the world as he develops his independence.

190-191 • Austria. A palomino-coated Haflinger coat seems to draw a sense of security from his mother's proximity.

191 • France. While his mother feeds, the small Arabian remains close by; he is almost fearful.

192 and 193 ● France. With its mother, the foal learns to distinguish edible herbs.

194-195 ● Great Britain. A tiny Shetland plays with his mother, helping to develop his muscles.

196 ● France. The mother-child bond is very strong among horses.

197 ● Asia. Mother and foal of the Przewalski breed in a pose of tender "complicity."

USA. Two foals rest happily in a soft, grassy meadow. A foal's life includes wild, scatty gallops and deep sleeps.

200-201 ● Iceland. This little Iceland pony doesn't seem to want to wander far from his mother.

201 ● Great Britain. A young Shetland pony comfortably asleep in a field.

202-203 ● Austria. The foals of many species – in this case a Haflinger – gradually lose the down they have when they are born.

Great Britain. Two colts play freely: moments like these help to teach them jumping movements.

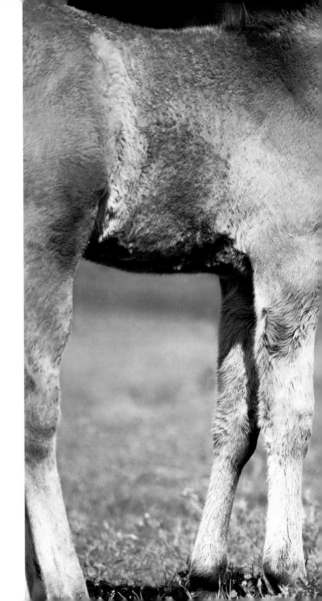

● Great Britain. A pair of foals
frolics close to the adults of the
herd; they gaze at each other,
discovering the world around
them together.

208 and 209 • Germany. The first neighs of two very young foals: communication is fundamental in the animal world.

210-211 • Iceland. This Iceland pony seems to be hiding behind his mother's reassuring bulk.

USA. A foal trots and then rests in a colorful field.

214 and 215 ● Great Britain. Foals need constant contact with the adults in the herd.

216-217 ● Germany. A Shetland pony adopts the most extreme – and comical – way to scratch its back.

• Germany. Two foals concentrate on cleaning themselves. Their sense of touch is so highly
developed that even a fly landing anywhere on their body is enough to trigger a reaction.

220 ● USA. Long, slender legs, clearly out of proportion to their bodies, help foals move with a minimum of agility and speed.

221 ● France. An Appaloosa cares for and cleans his coat.

222 ● Great Britain. A baby Gypsy Vanner stretches his legs in playful jumps next to an adult.

223 ● Great Britain. A lovely dappled colt bucks energetically, its movements showing remarkable natural elegance.

Germany. A Friesian colt, already looking as haughty as an adult of the breed, stands near its mother.

Great Britain. On the left, an Arabian looks at a kitten; on the right, a Shetland pony curiously watches an egret.

228 ● Great Britain. A tranquil trot for these colts that are familiarizing themselves
with the world around them.

229 ● Ireland. The mother of a tiny Irish pony teaches her youngster to run
in the open space.

“THE CONDITION OF FOALS IS SINGULAR, AS THEY ARE THE GAWKY OFFSPRING OF WHAT WE PERCEIVE AS THE MOST GRACEFUL CREATURES ON EARTH. THIS MAKES THEM ALL THE MORE TOUCHING TO OBSERVE AS THEY DETERMINEDLY FOLLOW THEIR PARENTS' EXAMPLE TO FACE WHAT WE CAN EASILY DEFINE AS A METAMORPHOSIS RATHER THAN NORMAL GROWTH. ”

● Great Britain. Two colts enjoy their contact with nature in complete solitude.

232 ● Germany. There is a long tradition of breeding Arabian foals: the Bedouins considered them a priceless treasure.

233 ● Germany. Arabian foals show all the breed's sense of pride and elegance, but on a smaller scale.

● Germany. A mother lavishes care and attention on her foal. As a rule, horses are extremely affectionate and sensitive: "friendly" in the full sense of the word.

USA. A Criollo mother and foal nuzzle each other affectionately. These are very sturdy and reliable horses that are used to the open spaces of the pampas.

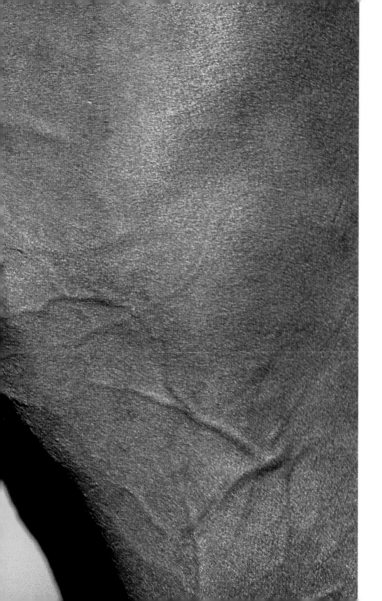

USA. An Arabian foal suckles his mother. After the birth, a foal will normally be able to stand within an hour, and the first thing he does is to drink his mother's rich milk.

240-241 • Great Britain. A gray-coated Arabian lavishes attention on her bay foal. The rarest color for foals of this breed is all black.

242-243 • Great Britain. An entire family runs in the meadow: this is an excellent exercise for the growth of young foals and fillies.

244 • Germany. Foals communicate on various levels. Even the position of their ears, erect and relaxed as here, is significant.

245 • Germany. The sense of smell is the most important one in social relations among foals. As they smell, they often raise their upper lip slightly.

246 ● Great Britain. An Arabian colt seeks shelter under his mother's belly.

247 ● Germany. Ponies often turn to their mothers, as they seek their attention for something or simply want to run and frolic.

● Iceland. A small Iceland pony tries every position imaginable to rest. Here, though the pony seems to be grazing, it is actually dozing.

MUZZLES and WHINNIES

GABRIELE BOISELLE

251 ● Iceland. The Palomino pony almost looks angry. In reality, this kind of grimace is referred to as the Flehman reflex, and it is connected with olfactory perception.

253 ● Austria. Haflingers are generally very gentle by nature but during the mating season aggressiveness and fighting is seen more frequently.

INTRODUCTION Muzzles and Whinnies

My PROFESSION AS A PHOTOGRAPHER BRINGS ME CLOSER TO MORE DIFFERENT TYPES OF HORSE THAN ALMOST ANYBODY ELSE CAN HOPE TO MEET. THERE ARE THE TIMID ONES AND THE RUDE ONES, THE ARROGANT ONES AND THE "MACHOS." I CAN NEVER TELL WHICH CHARACTER WILL POP UP IN FRONT OF MY LENS. AND I AM ALWAYS ANXIOUSLY LOOKING FORWARD TO DISCOVER GREAT NEW PERSONALITIES ON MY PHOTO-SHOOTS – AND MOST OFTEN SUCCEED. SOMETIMES I REALLY HAVE TO WATCH OUT. ONCE I PHOTOGRAPHED ANSATA NILE PASCHA, A WELL-REGARDED CHAMPION ARABIAN STALLION. THIS VERY SPECIAL HORSE HAD SEEN IT ALL, ALL THE SHOW RINGS OF THE WORLD,

INTRODUCTION Muzzles and Whinnies

BOTH SIDES OF THE OCEAN IN AMERICA AND EUROPE. HE WAS JUST FED UP WITH ALL THE CRUELLY BURDEN-SOME DEMANDS OF THE TRAINERS AND WAS BEGGING TO BE A NORMAL HORSE OUT IN THE FIELD. BUT BEING TO VALUABLE HE HAD TO GO TO WORK AND HATED IT. AND HE HATED ALL THE PEOPLE WEARING DRESSED UP IN WHITE FOR A PERFORMANCE OR STRUTTING AROUND CARRYING A WHIP IN THEIR HANDS. UNFORTU-NATELY, THAT DAY I WAS IN WHITE WITH MY CAMERA IN MY HAND – AND THAT DID NOT LOOK GOOD TO THE STALLION. SO HE CAME TOWARD, EYES BLAZING, TEETH BARED. FOR A MOMENT, MY BREATHING FROZE; I KNEW I WOULD NOT BE FAST ENOUGH TO ESCAPE THROUGH THE FENCE. TRUSTING TO THE INSTINCTS I HAD DEVE-

INTRODUCTION Muzzles and Whinnies

LOPED WITH HORSES, I DID NOT WAIT UNTIL HE HAD REACHED ME, BUT SPRANG FORWARD TOWARD HIM LIKE AN ATTACKING FORCE. HE WAS SO TAKEN BY SUR-PRISE THAT HE JUMPED ASIDE, STOPPED AND TURNED AROUND WITH AN EXPRESSIONLESS FACE, ASKING "WHAT WAS THAT??? THEN HE CAREFULLY STEPPED CLOSER, AS IF ASKING "HALLO! WHO ARE YOU?" SO, I HAD BROKEN HIS BARRIER OF HATE. I PUT MY CAMERA ASIDE AND WE PLAYED AROUND FOR ABOUT HALF AN HOUR IN THE PASTURE – HE HAD FUN WITH ME. HE WAS ONE OF THE MOST PERFECT MODELS I HAVE EVER HAD AND AS GENTLE AND COOPERATING AS YOU COULD IMAGINE . . . SO LONG AS NONE OF HIS TRAINERS SHOWED UP. I'VE LEARNED ONE LESSON IN MY JOB:

Muzzles and Whinnies

Introduction

NEVER TRUST THE WORD OF PEOPLE ABOUT HORSES. YOU MUST YOURSELF DISCOVER THE MAKE-UP OF THE HORSE IN FRONT OF YOU: INSIDE AND OUTSIDE. AND I NEVER FOUND A REALLY MEAN HORSE THAT WAS NOT MADE MEAN BY MAN. HORSES ARE THE MOST NOBLE AND SPIRITUAL CREATURES I HAVE EVER MET IN MY LIFE. I HAVE SEEN HORSES BEATEN UP AND MISTREATED YET STILL FAITHFUL AND LOYAL. I HAVE SEEN HORSES CARING FOR THEIR HANDICAPPED RIDERS, LIKE FOR THEIR OWN CHILDREN. I AM BLESSED TO BE ABLE TO DISCOVER THE WORLD OF HORSES AGAIN AND AGAIN, TO LEARN SO MUCH ABOUT THEM – AND TO ADORE THEM MORE AND MORE.

- Iceland. Iceland ponies being demonstrative. Horses are social animals and hate to be alone.

Argentina. Criollo stallions fiercely defending their mares. The winner will lead the entire herd.

Argentina. Determined
and independent, Criollo
stallions have a very
strong character amply
demonstrated in their
"fiery" behavior.

Argentina. A Criollo stallion demonstrates his physical strength.

Germany. A bay and sorrel use their physical strength trying
to defeat one another.

Austria. Two Haflingers battle to win the leadership of the herd. In this struggle, each horse tries to defeat the other, using its robust jaws and kicking with its front legs in the attempt.

268 ● France. The bay clearly seems to have got the better of his adversary.

269 ● The Netherlands. Fighting between horses, Friesians in this case, may not be "to the death," but can nevertheless be violent.

270 ● Austria. A dramatic fight between two Haflinger ponies.

271 ● The Netherlands. A Friesian expresses the sheer joy of freedom with spontaneous enthusiasm.

272 ● Ireland. Gypsy Vanners are athletically built, which makes them well suited to riding and dressage.

272-273 ● Great Britain. Bred horses, in this case a Gypsy Vanner, need just as much freedom and open space as their wild cousins.

● Iceland. Two Iceland ponies show their teeth in an act of defiance. If tamed early, this breed is very gentle.

France. A horse from the Camargue seems to have relished its meal. Wild horses eat only a little at a time, but often.

278-279 ● Egypt. An Arabian energetically scratches its back in the dust.

279 ● The Netherlands. A black Friesian finds relief from the insects by rolling on the ground.

● Spain. Andalusian horses rub against a tree trunk. Regardless of where they live, horses must deal with an ever-present torment: insects.

France.
France. A stockade
becomes a welcome
source of relief for this
wild horse tormented by
itchiness.

Italy. These horses behave tenderly toward each other during the courting season.

● Spain.
Two Spanish horses
show affectionate
behavior. This breed, with
a noble appearance and
character, is very strong
and athletic and can be
tamed with great ease.

288 ● Iceland. Two Iceland ponies seek contact with each other.

289 ● Hungary. Shagya Arabians are tender towards one another.

Austria. Horses detest solitude, so they are often seen side by side in pairs, like these two Haflingers.

LIFE on the RANCH

MEDFORD TAYLOR

• USA. A cowboy and his horse show off in a wild vault.

INTRODUCTION Life on the Ranch

"YEE HA! . . . HERE THEY COME." DISTANT HOOFBEATS BREAK THE DAWN ON ASSATEAGUE IS-LAND, VIRGINIA. SUDDENLY, FROM OUT OF THE FOG HANGING LOW OVER THE SALT MARSHES AND DUNES, HORSES APPEAR, POUNDING THEIR WAY ACROSS THE SAND. ON THIS JULY MORNING, "SALTWATER" COW-BOYS MOVE THE NORTHERN HERD OF WILD HORSES TOWARD THE OCEAN FOR A TWO-MILE TROT ALONG THE BEACH AND THEN THE CHANNEL SWIM TO CHIN-COTEAGUE. THIS IS THE START OF THE ANNUAL PONY PENNING. DURING ONE WEEK EVERY YEAR, A GROUP OF MEN FROM A VARIETY OF PROFESSIONS MEET UP FOR THE WILD HORSE ROUNDUP. AND FOR THIS BRIEF

• Italy. A Tuscan hand tends the herd.

INTRODUCTION Life on the Ranch

TIME IN SUMMER THEY BECOME SALTWATER COW-
BOYS, AND PARTICIPATE IN A TRADITIONAL ROUNDUP
THAT HAS LASTED FOR NEARLY 80 YEARS. 'I GREW UP
DREAMING OF BEING A COWBOY AND LOVING THE
COWBOY WAYS . . . PURSUING THE LIFE OF MY HIGH-
RIDING HEROES.' THESE WORDS, FROM THE WILLIE
NELSON SONG "MY HEROES HAVE ALWAYS BEEN COW-
BOYS," COULD BE THE DREAM OF EVERY BOY WHO
GREW UP GOING TO COWBOY MOVIES AS I DID. WEAR-
ING MY TOY SIX-GUNS, I WOULD RELIVE THE MOVIE ON
MY WALK BACK HOME FROM THE THEATER, IN THE
SOUTHERN TOWN WHERE I GREW UP. MANY YEARS
LATER AS A PHOTOGRAPHER ON ASSIGNMENT, I LAY
ON MY SWAG UNDER THE STARS OF THE AUSTRALIAN
OUTBACK . . . ON A REAL CATTLE MUSTER, WITH REAL

INTRODUCTION Life on the Ranch

COWBOYS . . . RINGERS, DOWN UNDER, MATE. I WAS AT PEACE . . . A BOYHOOD DREAM COME TRUE.

THE CREATION OF THE MYTHIC COWBOY PERSONA BY POPULAR CULTURE IS NOT CONFINED TO THE AMERICAN COWBOY – THE COWBOY IS A UNIVERSALLY ADMIRED LEGEND. IN MEXICO, HE'S CALLED VAQUERO. THE *GAUCHOS* OF ARGENTINA, URUGUAY AND BRAZIL STILL RIDE PROUDLY; ONCE CALLED THE 'WANDERERS OF THE PAMPAS,' *GAUCHOS* ARE A RESPECTED SYMBOL OF THEIR COUNTRIES HERITAGE. IN AUSTRALIA THE COWBOYS ARE RINGERS, JACKAROOS AND JILLAROOS, AND THEY LIVE AN INDEPENDENT AND RUGGED EXISTENCE. THE BUTTERO IS ITALY'S COWBOY. ALONG CENTRAL ITALY'S WESTERN BORDERS, IN TUSCANY, LIES THE HIDDEN FRONTIER OF MAREMMA. AN ALMOST

INTRODUCTION Life on the Ranch

MYTHICAL PLACE OF OPEN PLAINS AND FORESTS, MAREMMA IS HOME TO THE LAST OF THE BUTTERI. THERE ARE FEW WILD HORSES OR CATTLE LEFT, BUT MANY OF THE BUTTERI'S TRADITIONS ARE KEPT ALIVE THROUGH EVENTS SPONSORED BY BUTTERI D'ALTA MAREMMA, INCLUDING THE ANNUAL TRANSHUMANCE, A TWO-DAY WILD-HORSE ROUNDUP ACROSS THE TUS-CAN LANDSCAPE.

A COWBOY AND HIS HORSE ARE AS ONE. TOGETHER THEY DO A JOB. THEY WORK AS A TEAM THROUGH DRIVING RAIN, DUST STORMS, BLIZZARDS OR BAKING SUN. A COWBOY LOVES HIS HORSE BECAUSE HE IS LOYAL AND CARRIES HIM THROUGH THE BEST AND THE WORST OF TIMES, AND HE IS ALWAYS DILIGENT, NO MATTER HOW TIRED FROM HOURS UNDER THE SAD-

INTRODUCTION Life on the Ranch

DLE. A CENTURY AGO, A COWBOY AND HIS HORSE COULD RIDE THOUSANDS OF MILES ON ONE CATTLE DRIVE. TODAY THE AMERICAN WEST HAS BOUNDARIES, FENCES AND INTERSTATE HIGHWAYS. CATTLE ARE MOVED IN TERMS OF DAYS, NOT WEEKS OR MONTHS. IN AUSTRALIA, RINGERS NOW TAKE A FEW DAYS TO DRIVE CATTLE TO THE ROAD TRAINS, WHERE BEFORE IT WOULD TAKE WEEKS TO REACH A RAILHEAD. THE COWBOY'S WAY OF LIFE HAS CHANGED JUST LIKE EVERYONE ELSE'S. BUT FOR THE REST OF US, IT IS THE COWBOY'S WAY OF LIFE THAT WE ADMIRE. IT IS THEIR LIFE THAT WE ROMANTICIZE ABOUT, BECAUSE A COW-BOY REPRESENTS INDEPENDENCE, ADVENTURE AND WIDE OPEN SPACES. A VAQUERO, *GAUCHO*, BUTTERO, JACKAROO, OR BUCKAROO — THEY ARE PART OF

Life on the Ranch

Introduction

EACH COUNTRY'S HERITAGE, AND WE LOVE THEM FOR THEIR TENACITY TO SURVIVE IN CHANGING TIMES. BACK ON CHINCOTEAGUE, THE COLTS AND YEARLINGS HAVE BEEN SOLD AT AUCTION, AND THE SALTWATER COWBOYS DRIVE THE HORSES DOWN NARROW STREETS OF THIS ISLAND TOWN. THEY'RE HEADING BACK TO THE WATER TO SWIM THE CHANNEL HOME TO ASSATEAGUE ISLAND. WET COATS GLISTEN IN THE SUN AS THEY RISE FROM THE WATER AND THEIR HOOVES HIT FAMILIAR SAND AND MUD. WATCHING THE HORSES SHAKE THEIR MANES AND RUN FREE AGAIN YOU CAN ONLY HAVE A FEELING OF GRATITUDE, KNOWING THE HERD WILL STILL BE THERE NEXT YEAR WHEN THE SALTWATER COWBOYS RETURN.

- Argentina. Getting a herd across a river is a tough job: horses are delicate animals.

USA. Shoeing a horse requires skill and precision.

304-305 ● USA. The lasso is an everyday work tool for a cowboy.

305 ● USA. Keeping a herd of wild horses under control requires constant movement.

306-307 • USA. Horses are led into the enclosure.

307 • USA. The animals on a ranch are kept clean and healthy.

308 and 308-309 ● USA. Enclosure gates are made from simple poles that can be lifted out of the ground.

310-311 ● USA. Two cowboys break into a gallop in front of the mountains of Utah.

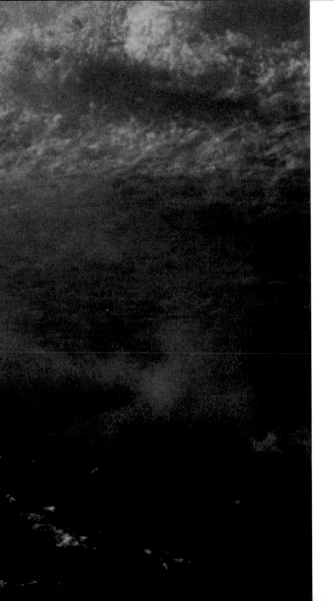

USA. A hand leads the herd as he loops his lasso in the air.

USA. A racing group of wild horses is a breathtaking sight.

316 ● USA. Boots and spurs are typical wear for cowboys.

316-317 ● USA. Other important pieces of clothing are suede leg protectors called chaps.

Canada. A blacksmith forges horseshoes in the semidarkness of his workshop. Life on the ranch follows age-old rhythms.

USA. Horses are of major
importance in controlling herds
of cattle.

USA. Working with horses not only requires strength but also qualities such as sensitivity and awareness.

324 and 325 ● USA. In addition to being capable and courageous riders, cowboys must also be very agile and have great manual ability in order to handle the lasso correctly.

326-327 ● USA. A group of horses gallops freely outside the pen.

328-329 ● USA. The herd is checked every day, rain or shine.

from 330 to 335 ● USA. Canyons, cowboys and wild horses are iconic images of the American West and its untrammeled freedoms.

336-337 ● USA. Working in pairs makes following the animals easier.

338-339 ● USA. Watched over by a herder, the livestock move on in an orderly manner.

340-341 ● USA. Wide open spaces and the open sky are appealing traits of the cowboy's work

from 342 to 345 ● USA. A vigilant eye needs to be kept when the herd is grazing or in the ring.

346 and 347 ● USA. Cowboys and horses have a hard time picking their way through the fresh snow. The Pinto, Quarterhorse and Appaloosa are the breeds preferred by cowboys because of their stamina and docile temperament.

348-349 ● USA. Cowboys have to handle the harshness of nature and the elements.

350-351 ● Argentina. Led by the *gaucho*, who is barely visible in the upper part of the picture, a herd of Criollos briskly fords a torrent on the pampa.

from 352 to 355 ●
Argentina. *Gauchos*
watch the herd from
behind for a better view.

Mexico. Lasso in hand to intimidate the cattle, the herdsmen rides along at the edge of the herd, close enough to keep it from dispersing.

358 ● Argentina. Criollos are difficult to train, and the presence of an already trained one often helps the process.

359 ● Argentina. Two *domadores* at work in the pen.

360-361 ● Argentina. The *domador*, who faces serious risks in his work, is a highly respected figure.

362-363 ● Argentina. Two *gauchos* recover a calf in difficulty.

363 and 364-365 ● Argentina. Fording rivers is a dramatic moment, often dangerous for men and horses.

366-367 ● Argentina. Two *gauchos* steer a herd of Criollos by whirling short crops called *rebenques*.

368 and 369 ● Italy. Tuscany's superb countryside is a fitting backdrop to these working herders.

370-371 ● Italy. Like other herdsmen around the world, the *butteri* work with horses every day, developing a very special rapport of equality and friendship.

"FOR HERDSMEN AROUND THE WORLD AND THOSE WHO LIVE WITH LIVESTOCK EVERY DAY, THE HORSE MEANS WORK, FATIGUE AND SWEAT – RAIN OR SHINE – AND SLEEPING OUT IN THE OPEN. AT THE SAME TIME, HOWEVER, IT ALSO IMPLIES THE KIND OF FREEDOM DREAMED BY MANY AND ENJOYED BY FEW.**"**

from 372 to 375 ● Italy. In the Maremma, the *butteri*'s horse is accustomed to living semi-wild in the country, alongside the longhorn cattle typical of the region.

● Italy. The first step in training the Maremmana is handled without a saddle, working inside the pen.

378-379 ● France. The *gardians*, the herdsmen of the Camargue, follow a young bull. The cattle are raised in freedom in order to run during the traditional festivals of Provence.

380-381 ● France. A group of *gardians* precedes a large herd of cattle of the Camargue. The man in the middle grips the tool of this trade, the long handle of the *trident*.

Spain. A *doma vaqueras* follows the herd, which moves at rapid speed.

● Hungary. The thrilling spectacle of the *czikos*, the highly skilled Hungarian herdsmen, enlivens the *puszta*'s monotonous landscape.

● Hungary. A *czikos*, dressed in the traditional oversized blue shirt, guides a herd of magnificent bays across the *puszta*.

from 388 to 391 •
Mongolia. Mongolian
stockhands have to
brave very low
temperatures in wide
open spaces.

- Australia. The Australian working cowboy's environment is usually huge, dry, dusty expanses.

394-395 ● Australia.
A boat and cable are vital
tools is bringing this
horse across a broad
river.

396-397 ● Australia.
The cowboys' gait slows
up to match that of their
herds. It reflects the
traditional – or "natural " –
tempo of their calling.

Australia. Sun and dust accompany the herdsmen's daily work. In Australia, cowboys are referred to by various names, such as *jackaroos*, *jillaroos*, or *ringers*.

CHILDREN and HORSES

PAOLO MANILI

• India. A very young Buddhist novice looks after a Mongolian horse.

INTRODUCTION Children and Horses

Not all children like horses. Some are frightened of their size or, more simply, they prefer other animals like dogs, cats and rabbits, etc. On the other hand, there are children who like horses before they have even seen one. This attraction may result from their education, children's stories, cartoons or simply their own character. Such children are extraordinarily interested in horses and, when they first encounter one, an alchemy occurs that not even experts are able to define. This fascination is returned by horses that recognize that the young humans before them are not predators to flee but simply the 'foals' of another species.

INTRODUCTION Children and Horses

IN ONE OF THE MYSTERIOUS LAWS OF NATURE, OFTEN EVEN SKITTISH HORSES ARE ATTENTIVE AND SHOW DELICACY TOWARD CHILDREN. THIS EXTRAORDINARY ANIMAL EXERTS A STRONG APPEAL ON PEOPLE, IN PARTICULAR THOSE WITH GREAT IMAGINATION: THE 'NOBLE QUADRUPED' CELEBRATED BY ARTISTS REPRESENTS BEAUTY AND GRACE, STRENGTH AND HUMAN DREAMS. THEY STIMULATE THE IMAGINATION, DESIRE AND THE DESIRE FOR POSSESSION. CHILDREN LOVE BEAUTY, THEY DREAM WITH OPEN EYES, WANTING THINGS THAT THEY LIKE. THEN, ONCE THEIR INTEREST IS RECIPROCATED, A LOVE SWELLS INSIDE THEM FOR THIS LARGE, APPRECIATIVE CREATURE, SO FRIENDLY THAT IT MIGHT BE A GIANT TOY. THIS SIMILARITY TO A TOY HAS BEEN TAKEN AS THE

Children and Horses

Introduction

BASIS FOR THE MOST RECENT METHOD OF TEACHING VERY YOUNG CHILDREN TO RIDE. IN COUNTRIES WHERE EQUESTRIANISM IS ADVANCED, CHILDREN START TO LEARN RIDING ON PONIES RATHER THAN HORSES FOR A MORE BALANCED RELATIONSHIP BETWEEN SIZE AND STRENGTH, AND THEY APPROACH COMPETITIVE RIDING THROUGH PONY GAMES. IN THE WEST PONY-RIDING COMPETITIONS ARE VERY COMMON AND EVEN HAVE AN INTERNATIONAL CALENDAR; THE BEST RIDERS ARE ELIGIBLE TO ENTER EUROPEAN AND WORLD CHAMPIONSHIPS IN VARIOUS DISCIPLINES AND ARE LIKELY TO GO ON TO BECOME FUTURE CHAMPIONS.

405 • USA. A young rider carefully guides her pet to the ranch.

406-407 • USA. A budding cowboy simulates a rodeo performance under the eyes of a 'real' cowboy.

408 ● USA. Whether made of wood or of real flesh and blood, a horse is a perfect play companion.

409 ● USA. Tackling the rudiments of lassoing.

410-411 ● USA. Before a rodeo, a young boy watches a horse with evident admiration.

● USA. Youngsters together:
a boy and a colt gain confidence
as they study each other with
interest.

● Germany. A young rider shows her confidence in her magnificent Arabian. More than with other domesticated animals, human beings tend to treat horses as equals.

416 ● USA. An aspiring cowgirl in a matching outfit tenderly kisses her proud steed.

417 ● Ireland. A girl and a pony get to know one another. Horses love to be petted.

USA. Once initial wariness is dissolved (mostly caused by the difference in size), children place complete trust in horses – a trust that will not be betrayed.

Great Britain. The woolly shin-bones of a Shire are as tall as the squatting girl but she is not in any danger. Even the most skittish horses treat children with care.

422 • Great Britain. Two young jockeys jump a hedge during a competition.

423 • Great Britain. Falls are educational: a jockey slips from his saddle as he comes out of a jump.

424 ● Italy. An aspiring jockey dismounts, with some difficulty, from the saddle.

424-425 ● Great Britain. The enthusiasm of young riders – and their ponies – is unleashed at the gallop during a gymkhana.

426 ● Great Britain. Wearing a cap and
with her plaits in ribbons, a young girl
waits for the start of a competition.

426-427 ● Great Britain. Jumping with
style: learning is best done early.

428 and 429 ● Mongolia. Numbered participants at a horse-race in Mongolia prepare to start. The riders chosen are between 5 and 13 years of age because this ensures the ability of the horses is tested, not that of the riders.

430-431 ● Mongolia. Children and adults in the saddle of impressive young Mongolian horses accelerate into a gallop on the steppes.

HORSES in UNIFORM

HENRY DALLAL

Great Britain. On the Queen's Birthday, celebrated in June, the troops of the Household
Cavalry (the Queen's personal guard) draw near to Windsor Castle.

INTRODUCTION Horses in Uniform

New to London, I was awakened by the echoing sounds of some thirty horses trotting in the cobblestone streets of this city. Running over to the window, the sight and the sounds of the "four-legged soldiers" with their mounted troopers on "watering orders" in the early morning darkness sparked fascination in me. Thus began my journey to photograph the Household Cavalry Mounted Regiment, the British Sovereign's ceremonial bodyguard, the elite of the world's mounted cavalry. Some 23,000 images later, with my book *PAGEANTRY AND PERFORMANCE* completed, I remained just as fascinated as when I first started this journey seven years ago. Britain is world-

INTRODUCTION Horses in Uniform

RENOWNED IN KEEPING ALIVE THE TRADITION OF THE WARHORSE OF YESTERYEAR IN ITS BRILLIANT POMP AND CEREMONY. WE HAVE THE HOUSEHOLD CAVALRY, THE KING'S TROOP ROYAL HORSE ARTILLERY, THE HONOURABLE ARTILLERY COMPANY, AND NUMEROUS OTHER UNITS, AS WELL AS THE ROYAL MEWS (STABLES) WITH ITS MUSEUM. SOME OTHER COUNTRIES ALSO MAINTAIN THE TRADITION OF THE "UNIFORMED HORSE," WEAVING IT IN THEIR CULTURE AND HISTORY. THERE IS THE GARDE REPUBLICAIN IN FRANCE, THE PRESIDENT'S BODY GUARD IN PAKISTAN, AND IN INDIA THE 61ST CAVALRY, AND IN CANADA THE ROYAL CANADIAN MOUNTED POLICE. THE CLOSER I LOOKED AT THE HORSE, THE MORE THERE WAS TO SEE AND MARVEL AT. BESIDES ITS SOFT VELVETY MUZZLE, EVERY

INTRODUCTION Horses in Uniform

HORSE HAS ITS INDIVIDUAL CHARACTER, PERSONALITY AND TEMPERAMENT. ON THE DAY OF AN EVENT SUCH AS THE QUEEN'S BIRTHDAY PARADE, AN 'ARMADA' OF OVER 400 HORSES COME TO DUTY AND TOGETHER WITH THEIR MOUNTED RIDERS (WHO AS MODERN SOLDIERS MAY HAVE JUST RETURNED FROM A BATTLE ZONE OR PEACE-KEEPING DUTY) RADIATE THAT GALLANTRY AND A SENSE OF PRIDE AND HONOR. EACH HORSE HAS BEEN TRAINED FOR MONTHS, AND ON THAT DAY, GROOMED FOR HOURS. THEIR HOOFS HAVE BEEN POLISHED; THE SOLES OF THEIR FEET POWDERED WITH WHITE CHALK. TROOPER AND HORSE ARE BRIGHTLY UNIFORMED WITH HEAVY SADDLES AND AC-COUTERMENTS, JUST AS IN DAYS OF CAVALRY BATTLES. THE CRISP EARLY MORNING LIGHT, THE MIST, THE HORSES'

INTRODUCTION Horses in Uniform

WARM BREATH VISIBLE IN THE AIR, ARE ALL PART OF THE EX-
PECTANCY. THE JINGLING AND CLANGING, AND THE OCCA-
SIONAL COUGH OR NEIGH AS THIS ARMY STANDS PATIENT-
LY IN RANK AND FILE WHILE THE COMMANDER INSPECTS
EVERY HORSE AND MOUNTED SOLDIER, BONDED AS ONE
PROUD BEING WAITING TO GO ON PARADE TO ESCORT THE
SOVEREIGN, PROUD TO STEP FORWARD AND MARCH IN
FRONT OF THE WORLD. WHETHER PULLING THE HEAVY
GUNS OR THE ROYAL COACH THEY KNOW THE ROUTE, THE
MOMENT, AND THE SOLEMNITY OF THE OCCASION. THERE
IS A TIME TO PLAY AND BUCK, AND THERE IS THE REQUIRE-
MENT TO STAND AT ATTENTION FOR HOURS. A COMPLETE
MOUNTED ORCHESTRA MARCHES PAST IN PERFECT STEP,
THE MUSICIANS OBEYING THE CONDUCTOR'S BATON AS HE

Horses in Uniform

Introduction

RIDES ON THE LEAD HORSE. THE HEAVY KETTLE DRUMS RE-
VERBERATING WITH THE MUSIC'S BEAT, PLAYED BY A REINS-
FREE DRUMMER, CAN BE IN A DIFFERENT TEMPO TO THE
PACE OF THE MARCH. THROUGH THE LOUDLY CHEERING
AND CLAPPING CROWD, BELOW THE HELICOPTERS CIR-
CLING OVERHEAD, THE ARMADA OF NEARLY 400 HORSES
PROUDLY PERFORM, MAINTAINING THE STRICTEST DISCI-
PLINE. JUST OCCASIONALLY A PARTICULAR HORSE DE-
CIDES, REGARDLESS OF HIS RIDERS RANK OR TITLE, HAS IT
NO BUSINESS BEING IN THE ROYAL PROCESSION, AND THUS
BEGINS HIS OWN SOLO PARADE, USUALLY AT A SWIFTER
PACE AND IN A DIFFERENT DIRECTION, BUT EVENTUALLY TO
THE PLACE WHERE HE IS FED. . . .

• Italy. The horseback band of the Carabinieri parade down Via dei Fori Imperiali in Rome.

Great Britain

440-441 ● Great Britain. The Life Guards here are seen walking in a circle at the end of the parade.

441 ● Great Britain. Roll-call for the Life Guards: the horses and their riders are subjected to an exhausting discipline.

442 • Great Britain. A Horse Guard awaits orders.

442-443 • Great Britain. Saddles and harness as splendid as on the days of battle: everything must be perfect to honor the royal household.

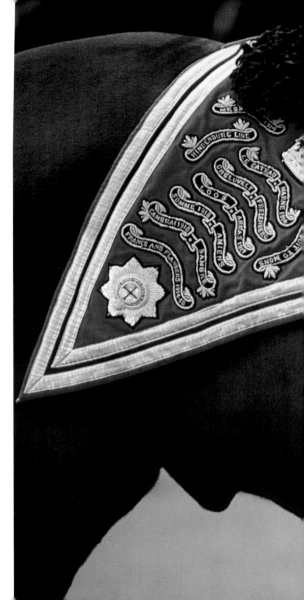

● Great Britain. Tiny details, like the shine on the boots and stirrups, receive a maximum amount of attention. Note the regimental monogram inscribed on the hoof.

● Great Britain. Wearing tunics embroidered with the Queen's monogram, musicians of the magnificent military band that accompanies the Trooping the Colour are able to play rhythms completely different to that of the march.

448-449 ● Great Britain. The Blues and Royals follow the Life Guards out of Windsor Castle.

449 ● Great Britain. Regiments assemble in Windsor Castle's vast Quadrangle.

Italy

- Italy. With the eternal Colosseum as a backdrop, the Carabinieri of the Cuirassier unit parade in Via dei Fori Imperiali during the Festa della Repubblica.

452 ● Italy. Drawn up in Piazza di Siena in Rome, the mounted Carabinieri await the start of the exciting Carosello.

453 ● Italy. Quadrilles of horseback Carabinieri perform changing formations during the Carosello, reproducing movements of troops in battle.

454-455 ● Italy. The Fanfara of the Carabinieri files past during the Festa della Repubblica in Rome.

Italy. A company of mounted Carabinieri break into a gallop in the park at Villa Borghese in Rome.

France

France. On July 14th, the festival that marks the fall of the Bastille, a sea of shiny helmets fills the Avenue des Champs Elysées. This is the Garde Republicaine on parade.

460 • France. The gleaming helmet of this Garde Républicaine cavalryman reflects the French sky.

461 • The Garde Républicaine's fanfare parades in front of the Louvre.

Spain

462 • Spain. A Spanish Civil Guard on service in the streets of Madrid.

462-463 • Spain. Horseback guards present their lances in Plaza de la Provincia in Madrid.

Sweden

464 ● Sweden. Trumpeters accompany the changing of the Swedish Royal Guards at the Royal Palace in Stockholm.

464-465 ● Sweden. The Swedish Royal Guard boasts the longest active service in the world: the regiment was formed in 1521.

Canada

466 • Canada. Wearing red worsted jackets, lancers of the Mounted Police prepare for a Musical Ride, in which 32 officers perform complex figures on horseback to military band music.

467 • Canada. Saddlecloths bear the monogram "MP", shorthand for the Royal Canadian Mounted Police.

● Canada. Units of horseback police (the famous Mounties) exhibit their skills at the gallop in a simulated charge in formation.

India

India. In New Delhi, units of the Presidential Guard maneuver in front of Rashtrapati Bhavan, the residence of the President of India.

from 472 to 475 ● India. Each year the Indian government invests large sums in the organization of the magnificent parades that celebrate the anniversary of the republic in the largest cities.

EQUESTRIAN SPORTS

PAOLO MANILI

- Great Britain. Polo requires daring, speed and skill by both horses and riders.

INTRODUCTION Equestrian Sports

IT IS THANKS TO EQUESTRIAN SPORTS THAT HORSES HAVE SURVIVED THE ADVENT OF THE COMBUSTION ENGINE. WITH THE LESSENING OF THEIR FUNCTIONS AS A MEANS OF TRANSPORT AND A WORKING ANIMAL, THEY ONLY REMAIN IN USE IN ARMIES FOR TRAINING PURPOSES AND EXHIBITIONS. IT IS FROM CAVALRY EXERCISES THAT MODERN THREE-DAY 'EVENTING' IS DERIVED (ALSO KNOWN AS HORSE TRIALS, CONCOURS COMPLET, AND MILITARY COMPETITION). IN EVENTING, A HORSE IS PUT THROUGH THREE SEPARATE TRIALS ON CONSECUTIVE DAYS: DRESSAGE IN THE RING, A CROSS-COUNTRY ENDURANCE WITH JUMPS, AND SHOW JUMPING. EVENTING IS AN INDIVIDUAL

• Switzerland. The White Turf is held each year in an unusual location for horseracing: the surface of the lake in St. Moritz.

INTRODUCTION Equestrian Sports

OLYMPIC SPORT ALONG WITH DRESSAGE AND SHOW-
JUMPING. THE FORMER, WHICH HAS ITS ORIGINS IN THE
RIDING SCHOOLS OF THE 17TH AND 18TH CENTURIES, IS
A DEMONSTRATION OF THE HORSE'S OBEDIENCE
THROUGH A SERIES OF MOVEMENTS PERFORMED IN-
SIDE A RECTANGLE OF PARTICULAR SIZE. SHOW-JUMP-
ING HAS COMPETITIONS OF A DIFFERENT NATURE AND
IS DERIVED FROM HUNTING: TO PROVE THE ABILITIES OF
A HORSE, THE ANIMAL WAS MADE TO JUMP BARRIERS
CONSTRUCTED TO RESEMBLE NATURAL OBSTACLES
FOUND IN THE COUNTRYSIDE. IT WAS BUT A SHORT
STEP FROM THIS TO THE ORGANIZATION OF COMPETI-
TIONS. THE BASIS OF THE MODERN TECHNIQUE –
WHICH WAS CODIFIED AT THE START OF THE 20TH CEN-

TURY BY CAPTAIN FEDERICO CAPRILLI OF THE ITALIAN CAVALRY AND INITIALLY TAUGHT AT THE PINEROLO SCHOOL – SPREAD AROUND THE WORLD. OTHER EQUESTRIAN SPECIALTIES ARE PRACTICED AT DIFFERENT LEVELS IN ALMOST ALL COUNTRIES, EACH WITH ITS OWN COMPETITION CALENDAR THAT INTEGRATES THE CONTINENTAL AND WORLD CHAMPIONSHIPS. FOR EXAMPLE, ENDURANCE RACES OVER DIFFERENT DISTANCES, ONE-, TWO- OR FOUR-HORSE HITCHES IN WHICH CARRIAGES ARE PULLED BY HORSES OVER COURSES TO DEMONSTRATE MANEUVERABILITY, AND VAULTING, IN WHICH A RIDER PERFORMS ARTISTIC AND GYMNASTIC MOVEMENTS WHILE THE HORSE IS MOVING IN A CIRCLE. THE LIST IS COMPLETED BY POLO, A SPORT

Equestrian Sports
Introduction

THAT ORIGINATED IN INDIA AND THAT THE BRITISH IM-
PORTED TO EUROPE, AND HORSE-BALL, WHICH IS A
SORT OF FOOTBALL ON HORSEBACK. THE OTHER HALF
OF THE EQUESTRIAN UNIVERSE IS REPRESENTED BY
WESTERN RIDING, INCLUDING CONTESTS THAT SIMU-
LATE WORK SITUATIONS, LIKE ROUNDING UP CATTLE ON
HORSEBACK. FROM THEIR ORIGIN AMONG THE NOBILI-
TY AND ELITE, EQUESTRIAN SPORTS HAVE BECOME IN-
CREASINGLY POPULAR AND WIDESPREAD, AND THUS
GIVEN A BOOST TO THE IMPROVEMENT OF HORSE-
BREEDING. RIDING IS ALSO A VERY 'MODERN' SPORT IN
WHICH MEN AND WOMEN COMPETE TOGETHER, WITH
THE LATTER OFTEN TAKING THE PRIZES.

● The Netherlands. Approaching the fence, horse and rider are in total harmony.

Showjumping

484 ● The Netherlands. At the 'top' of the jump, the horse seems suspended in the air.

485 ● Sweden. As the horse leaves the ground, the rider thrusts his weight forward to assist his mount in the jump.

Ireland. Once the jump is under way, the rest is up to the horse; the rider can no longer use the reins or whip to guide his mount.

488 • Ireland. Landing is the most difficult phase for the rider, and it is easy to lose balance and fall.

489 • Ireland. A 'messy' jump; the front legs are gathered unevenly toward the chest.

Scotland. The horse counts on its rider to manage the jump: the least uncertainty in the approach or on the rider's part and the horse refuses the jump.

from 492 to 495
Spain and Great Britain.
The fall of the horse, rider
or both usually carries a
heavy penalty and, in
certain competitions,
elimination.

Dressage

496 ● Spain. During the diagonal, the horse moves between opposite corners of the arena.

496-497 ● Spain. Elegance, balance, naturalness and perfect understanding: dressage is one of the noblest equestrian disciplines, as shown here.

498 ● Australia. At a walking pace, the horse moves with a measured but powerful gait.

499 ● Australia. Communication between horse and rider passes through the bit: the connection between the hands of the rider and the mouth of the horse is called 'contact.'

Australia. A strong emotional bond unites rider and horse. At the end of an Olympic dressage competition, a rider compliments her horse with a caress.

● Spain. Words and physical contact
  establish the fellowship required to
  attempt a dressage competition.

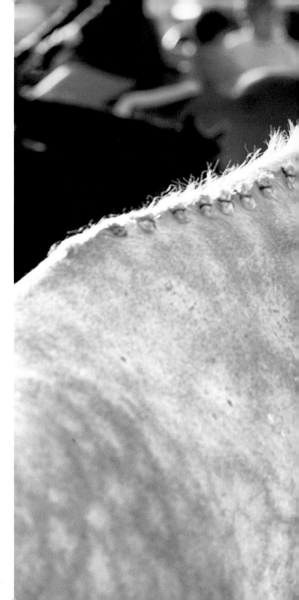

Polo

Switzerland. In the spectacular snow polo matches, players use a red ball, much larger than the traditional white ball.

● Switzerland. The famous Cartier
Polo World Cup is held in late
January on the frozen surface of
the St. Moritz lake.

Great Britain. Polo mallets are made from flexible malacca wood and are approximately 52 inches long.

510-511 ● USA. Polo horses have to have strong hocks to deal with the physical strain: often the animals are ponies rather than horses.

512-513 ● Great Britain. To prevent dangerous collisions in polo, complex rights govern precedence.

from 514 to 517 ● USA. Given the forcefulness of the game, hocks and shins are protected by pads to prevent excessive impact, but tails are also tied up to stop them getting tangled.

Trial

USA. The demanding Horse Trials are held over varied terrain with both artificial and natural obstacles, often with water.

Great Britain. Dramatic falls are not rare in Horse Trials.

Great Britain. Dealing with embankments requires great power going up and total control of the horse coming back down.

Great Britain. Frequent
falls require that the
horses' legs are well
protected with padding
and special ointments.

Great Britain. As the pair are racing against the clock, Horse Trials are based on speed rather than style.

Harness

● Great Britain. Harness racing includes different categories: singles, pairs, tandem driving (two horses in a row) and, as shown here, fours.

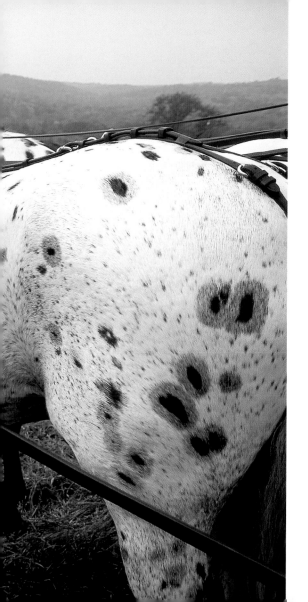

530-531 and 531 • Great Britain.
At harnesses races there is a delightful
air of yesteryear.

532-533 • Great Britain. In singles
driving, with a jockey and assistant,
notable speeds can be reached.

Trotting

from 534 to 541 •
Switzerland, Austria,
USA. Drivers in harness
racing or trotting races
sit in small, very light
metal gigs with rubber-
tired wheels known as
sulkies.

USA. The public identify competitors in harness racing by the colors the drivers wear.

Steeplechase

from 544 to 549 • Great
Britain, Ireland.
Steeplechasers require
exceptional strength to
tackle races over
distances of 3,000 meters,
jumping hedges, walls and
ditches.

● Great Britain, Ireland. Because steeplechase jumps cannot be moved, riders sometimes have to take 'to the air.'

Racing

from 552 to 555 •
Switzerland. A rider at full
gallop flies out of a cloud
of snow. This is the White
Turf in St. Moritz, a
sporting event that
combines international
trotting and galloping
races.

from 556 to 559 ● USA. Gates are needed to keep the chafing runners in line and apart. The instant they open, the horses unleash all their power in surging forward.

560-561 ● USA. Speed is not everything in a race. Depending on individual characteristics, there are 'fast' and 'slow'; horses: it is strategy not speed alone that wins races.

USA. Similar to the blasons of medieval riders, the colors the jockeys wear identify the horses' owners.

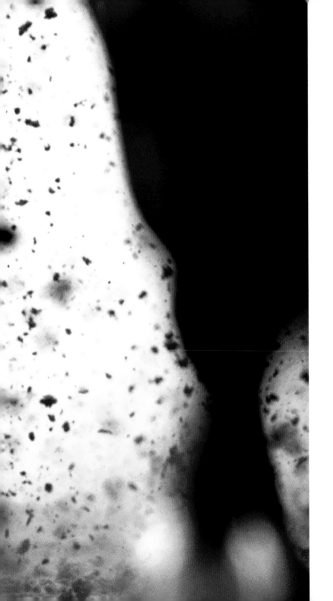

564-565 ● Spain.
Pineda race track in
Seville resounds to the
thunder of hooves.

566-567 ● China.
Saddle and harness are
reduced to the minimum
so the horses carry the
lightest weight possible.

568 ● Australia. This is the lead group in the Great Metropolitan Stakes in Randwick, Sydney, where races have been held since 1866.

569 ● Australia. Racehorses begin their training at the age of two. The best are soon entered in races, others begin at up to five years of age.

Great Bretain. Given the high speed on the track and flying divots of turf, jockeys wear goggles. Ventilation holes at the sides prevent the problem of fogging up.

572 ● Ireland. The Galway Races have been held since the 13th century.

572-573 ● Australia. To assist the horse's movements, the jockey leans forward, seldom in contact with the saddle.

574-575 ● Ireland. Horses exhibit their full power in the gallop.

576-577 ● USA. The public loves horseracing because of the beauty of horses at full gallop.

● Canada, Great Britain. Winners: a kiss for the horse is a demonstration of gratitude and affection.

The MAJOR SCHOOLS

PAOLO MANILI

- France. An instructor at the Cadre Noir School in Saumur, wearing a kepi and black uniform, directs a horse in a spectacular *cabriole*.

INTRODUCTION The Major Schools

In *HIPPARCHIKOS* ('CAVALRY OFFICER') WRITTEN IN 362 BC, XENOPHON REFERRED TO 'SCHOOL WORK' WHICH INVESTIGATED HARMONY OF MOVEMENT IN THE GAIT OF A HORSE. RIDING METHODS TAUGHT DURING THE RENAISSANCE TENDED TO EMPHASIZE EXECUTION OF MOVEMENTS BECAUSE AT THAT TIME FIREARMS HAD MADE ARMOR OBSOLETE AND THEREFORE GREATER MA-NEUVERABILITY WAS REQUIRED FROM HORSES. SINCE THEN, UP TILL THE PRESENT DAY RIDING HAS EVOLVED FROM THAT DEVELOPMENT. IN THE 16TH CENTURY RIDING WAS A 'CONSTRICTIVE' ACTIVITY, AT TIMES BRUTAL (LIKE THAT OF FEDERICO GRISONE, A PUPIL OF GIOVANBAT-

Austria. Like a flesh-and-blood equestrian monument, a Lipizzaner performs a *courbette* at the Spanish Riding School in Vienna.

INTRODUCTION The Major Schools

TISTA PIGNATELLI, WHO WAS MASTER OF THE RIDING SCHOOL OF NAPLES) DUE TO THE HEAVY AND 'COLD' TYPE OF HORSES USED. HOWEVER, THE EQUESTRIAN ARTS GRADUALLY INCREASED THE STYLIZATION OF THE MOVEMENTS OF A HORSE IN BATTLE UNTIL THEY DEVELOPED INTO THE REFINED MOVEMENTS TAUGHT TODAY IN RIDING SCHOOLS. DRESSAGE WAS EXALTED IN THE HIGH SCHOOL WHICH LED, IN THE 17TH CENTURY, TO THE HIGHLY REFINED TECHNIQUES PRACTICED BY PLUVINEL AND NEWCASTLE. FRANÇOIS ROBICHON DE LA GUERINIÈRE (1687–1751), THE FATHER OF FRENCH EQUESTRIANISM, TOOK RIDING TO THE FIRST, INCISIVE REVOLUTION, ONE THAT ATTEMPTED TO MEDIATE RIDING VIRTUOSITY WITH PRACTICALITY IN THE USE OF A HORSE. AFTER

INTRODUCTION The Major Schools

HIM, ACADEMIC RIDING CONTINUED TO DEVELOP UNTIL THE 19TH CENTURY WHILE HISTORICAL EVENTS DEMANDED A MORE VERSATILE USE OF SADDLE HORSES. AT THE START OF THE 20TH CENTURY, FEDERICO CAPRILLI (1868–1907), A CAPTAIN IN THE ITALIAN CAVALRY, CODIFIED THE 'NATURAL SYSTEM OF RIDING,' IN WHICH THE RIDER HAD TO ADAPT HIMSELF TO THE NATURAL BALANCES EXISTING IN THE HORSE'S GAIT RATHER THAN VICE VERSA. THIS WAS THE SECOND AND MORE FAR-REACHING REVOLUTION TO TAKE PLACE IN EQUESTRIANISM AND BECAME THE BASIS FOR MODERN RIDING TECHNIQUES. TAUGHT BY THE SCHOOL OF PINEROLO AND SOON SPREAD AROUND THE WORLD, PARTICULARLY WITH REGARD TO JUMPING, IT DISPENSED WITH THE STANDARD

The Major Schools
Introduction

RIDING TECHNIQUES TAUGHT. HOWEVER, SOME TRADITIONAL SCHOOLS HAVE SURVIVED TO THE PRESENT, FOR EXAMPLE THE SPANISH SCHOOL IN VIENNA (FOUNDED IN 1792 BY CHARLES V HABSBURG) AND THE SAUMUR SCHOOL IN FRANCE (FOUNDED IN THE MID-18TH CENTURY BY THE DUKE OF CHOISEUL). BOTH ARE 'SHRINES' TO HORSE RIDING AND REPRESENT AN INESTIMABLE TECHNICAL AND CULTURAL VALUE. IN ORDER THAT SPANISH TRADITIONS MIGHT BE PRESERVED, IN 1987 THE REAL ESCUELA ANDALUZA DEL ARTE EQUESTRE WAS FOUNDED IN JEREZ DE LA FRONTERA IN ANDALUSIA BY ALVARO DOMECQ ROMERO. THESE THREE ACADEMIES REPRESENT THE HISTORY OF HORSE RIDING.

- France. The name "Cadre Noir," applied to the Saumur school's officials, was later applied to the school itself. It comes from the color of the instructors' uniform.

LEAPING HORSES THAT CREATE FLESH-AND-BLOOD EQUESTRIAN MONUMENTS, HORSES THAT BUCK AND REAR WITH A SENSE OF ART AND PROPORTION, HORSES THAT DANCE: IT TAKES DISCIPLINE TO DO ALL THIS. AT THE TEMPLES OF THE ART OF RIDING, HOWEVER, MAN AND HORSE LEARN TOGETHER, AND IT IS THE FORMER WHO MUST ADAPT TO THE LATTER.

• Spain. An enthralling sequence in a *cabriole* in four consecutive photographs: only horses with perfectly trained rear muscles are capable of this exercise.

France. In the culminating phase of the *cabriole*, the horse, which is completely off the ground, kicks vigorously backwards.

France. The *croupade* is part of the so-called *Arie Alte*, i.e., the figures in which the horse lifts all four legs at the same time.

Real Escuela Andaluza del Arte Equestre

Jerez (Spain)

● Spain. Trainers at work at the Real Escuela Andaluza del Arte Ecuestre in Jerez de la Frontera: the renowned school's pride is the exhibition of How Andalusian Horses Dance, which leaves no doubt as to the excellence of the art practiced here.

596 ● Spain. The covered ring of the Picadero in Jerez de la Frontera is where the Real Escuela Andaluza del Arte Ecuestre has given its performances since 1987.

597 ● Spain. With its front legs high against its chest, a horse executes a *courbette*, a figure in which the animal makes small jumps forward balancing only on its hind legs.

Le Cadre Noir
in Saumur
France

● France. The 'career' of the Cadre Noir horses (shown here in a *croupade* and a *courbette*) lasts only about 15 years; they are then sold to other schools, breeders or private individuals.

● France. An elegant croupade at the Cadre Noir in Saumur. At the rider's command, the horse 'bucks', extending its rear legs completely.

602 and 603 • France. An instructor at the school in Saumur uses a long rein while training a horse to perform the *cabriole*.

604-605 • France. In the Cadre Noir riding school, two groups of five horses execute a *croupade* in sequence.

Spanische Reitschule Vienna

Austria

from 606 to 611 ● Austria. Most of the magnificent and highly trained horses at the Spanish Riding School in Vienna (Spanische Reitschule) are Lipizzaners.

HORSES on PARADE

SENIO SENSI

- New Zealand. A rodeo contestant shows skill and a sense of acrobatics in the saddle on an untamed horse.

INTRODUCTION Horses on Parade

THE LOVE FELT FOR HORSES IS SHOWN IN MANY PARTS OF THE WORLD BY THEIR MAJOR ROLE IN OUTSTANDING NATIONAL EVENTS AND CELEBRATIONS. WHETHER IT'S PARADES AND REVIEWS, MEDIEVAL PROCESSIONS, OR RACING, CULTURAL AND RECREATIONAL EVENTS, HORSES BRING SPLENDOR AND HONOR TO THEM WITH THEIR REGAL BEARING AND ABUNDANT ENERGY. FROM THE VIOLENT TWO- AND FOUR-HORSE CHARIOT RACES THAT ROUSED AUDIENCES IN ANCIENT ROME'S CIRCUSES, TO THE "ROMANTIC" TOURNAMENTS OF THE MIDDLE AGES, IN WHICH MAGNIFICENTLY ARMORED AND CAPARISONED HORSES SHARED THE GLORY WITH DUELING KNIGHTS,

● Italy. Since 1644, the year it was first run, Siena's Palio has been a major event for the citizens.

AND FROM POLO, PLAYED IN PERSIA OVER 1,000 YEARS AGO, TO PATO, A SORT OF HORSE-BORNE BAS-KETBALL INVENTED IN ARGENTINA AROUND 1600, HORSES HAVE BEEN INDISPENSABLE TO MANY TYPES OF RECREATION.

THEN THERE ARE RECENTLY INVENTED WESTERN COMPETITIONS LIKE BARREL RACING (A RACE BASED PRIMARILY ON SPEED AROUND A COURSE MARKED BY THREE BARRELS INSIDE A CORRAL), POLE BENDING (LIKE AN "EQUESTRIAN SLALOM" THROUGH A COURSE MARKED BY SEVEN POLES), AND OF COURSE THE FA-MOUS AND TRADITIONAL RODEOS, IN WHICH COW-BOYS ATTEMPT TO RIDE WILD HORSES.

EUROPE HAS SEVERAL EQUIVALENTS OF THE AMERI-

CAN COWBOYS: THE *CSIKOS*, OR HUNGARIAN STOCK-MEN, WHO PERFORM AMAZING STUNTS ON HORSE-BACK AT LOCAL SHOWS AND FAIRS, THE *GARDIENS* OF THE CAMARGUE, WHO ANNUALLY PARADE ON HORSE-BACK THROUGH THE STREETS OF ARLES DURING THE *FÊTE DES GARDIENS*, AND THE ITALIAN *BUTTERI*, WHO SHOW OFF THEIR RIDING SKILLS AT TRADITIONAL EVENTS LIKE THE MERCA IN MONTEROMANO, A FAIR THAT FOCUSES ON CATTLE BRANDING. THEN TOO, MENTION MUST BE MADE OF THE FAMOUS HORSE RACES ON SNOW AT ST. MORITZ IN SWITZERLAND, IN-AUGURATED IN 1984 AND SOON COPIED IN SIMILAR COMPETITIONS IN LECH (AUSTRIA) AND MÉGÈVE (FRANCE), AND THE FANTASIES IN MOROCCO, THE

INTRODUCTION Horses on Parade

MOST IMPORTANT OF WHICH IS HELD IN HONOR OF IDRIS I (THE FATHER OF THE NATION). AS EVENING FALLS, A MULTICOLORED CAVALRY SIMULATES A CHARGE, FIRING LONG-BARRELED, DECORATED AND SILVER-CHASED RIFLES INTO THE AIR. IN SPAIN HORSES TAKE PART IN LONG ESTABLISHED EVENTS: IN SEVILLE, FOR EXAMPLE, DURING THE FERIA IN APRIL, THE CITY FILLS WITH HORSES DECKED OUT IN FINE TRAPPINGS AND RIDERS IN THE TRADITIONAL COSTUME OF THE ANDALUSIAN FAIR, BOTH EQUALLY PROUD. AND IN MAY IN JEREZ THE FERIA DEL CABALLO IS THE FAVORITE OCCASION OF HORSE ENTHUSIASTS. THE CITY CAN ALSO BOAST THE REAL ESCUELA ANDALUZA DE ARTE ECUESTRE DI JEREZ, ONE OF THE

INTRODUCTION Horses on Parade

MOST RENOWNED RIDING SCHOOLS IN THE WORLD. IN ITALY THE SARTIGLIA OF ORISTANO HAS BEEN FAMOUS SINCE 1543; THIS IS A PARADE OF CAPARISONED HORSES RIDDEN BY MASKED HORSEMEN PERFORM-ING ELEGANT MANEUVERS.

BUT SURELY THE PERFECT COMBINATION OF MAN AND MOUNT TAKES PLACE IN SIENA AT THE PALIO. THIS EVENT IS A RACE OF THREE LAPS AROUND THE PIAZZA DEL CAMPO IN WHICH THE WINNER IS CONSIDERED TO BE THE HORSE, NOT THE RIDER. IN FACT, THE HORSE IS ABLE TO TAKE HIS CONTRADA (CITY QUARTER) TO VIC-TORY EVEN IF HIS RIDER HAS BEEN UNSEATED.

BEFORE THE RACE THE HORSES ARE BLESSED IN CHURCH AND, IN THE EVENT OF VICTORY, IS SEATED AT

Horses on Parade
Introduction

THE HEAD OF THE TABLE DURING THE CELEBRATORY FEAST THAT FOLLOWS. WATCHED OVER NIGHT AND DAY, THE HORSES UNLEASH THEIR NERVOUS ENERGY ON THE PIAZZA DEL CAMPO WHERE THEIR SAFETY AND WELL-BEING ARE GREATER THAN ANYWHERE ELSE IN THE WORLD.

WHEN THEY REACH OLD AGE, THEY ARE PENSIONED OFF IN A MEADOW AND, ON THEIR DEATH, THEY OFTEN RECEIVE THE TRIBUTE OF A TOMB AND DEATH NOTICE THAT DESCRIBES THEIR RACING PROWESS. IF I WERE A HORSE, I WOULD WANT TO RACE IN THE PALIO IN SIENA. AND I'M NOT THE ONLY ONE.

- Afghanistan. In a wild whirlwind of dust, a horde of riders attempts to win a goat. This is *Buskashi,* the Afghani national sport that boasts ancient origins.

Feria de Abril
Seville - Spain

622 ● Spain. During the Fería de Abril in Seville, the bright colors of flamenco costume offset the glossy coats of the horses.

622-623 ● Spain. Man and horse become a single unit when expressing Andalusian pride.

Spain. During the Fería in Seville, the horses' heads are adorned with floral ornaments.

Spain. On the first day of the Fería, which begins the week after Easter, participants arrive in the city on horseback or on carts pulled by twosomes or foursomes.

from 628 to 631 ● Spain. During the Feria de Abril, the gestures, poses and garb of a romantic and not-so-distant past are revived with powerful spontaneity.

Feria de Jerez
Jerez de la Frontera, Spain

632 and 633 ● Spain. Horses' tails embellished with bright ribbons: the decorations worn by the riders blend with the beauty of the animals at the Fería in Jerez.

from 634 to 637 ● Spain. The parade of the horses and carriages in the ring is a highlight of the Fería.

Fiesta de San Juan
Minorca - Spain

Spain. At the Fiesta di San Juan, which takes place in the streets of Minorca's old Muslim quarter, the horses move fearlessly through the crowd.

● Spain. The king of the Fiesta is the Minorcan horse, appreciated for vigor coupled with ridability.

Spain. During the Fiesta, the horses change their gaits in response to their riders' orders.

Luminarias
San Bartolomé de los Pinares
Spain

- Spain. A rider faces the flames with his horse, symbolically purifying the animal during the *Festival Luminarias* at San Bartolomé de los Pinares, in the province of Avila.

• Spain. The *Luminarias* festival is a religious celebration held on the night before St. Anthony's day, the patron saint of animals.

Palio di Siena
Italy

Italy. The Palio di Siena always arouses high excitement in the riders, the horses and the public.

Italy. Conveyed back to the height of the Middle Ages in the scene in the Piazza del Campo, the electrified audience follows the horserace. The event acquires an even more spectacular air as the pounding hooves throw up enveloping clouds of ocher earth.

Italy. During the Palio, the horses absolutely maximize their strength and stamina.

Sartiglia
di Oristano
Italy

● Italy. The Sartiglia di Oristano is a joust
instituted in 1543 to control the bloody
clashes that took place between the
Arborensi and Aragonesi.

Italy. In the *sartiglia* in Oristano (a game of Arabian-Iberian origin), riders perform a series of difficult exercises before the crowd.

● Italy. The riders in Oristano perform acrobatic tricks like the human pyramid,
the 'bridge' or the 'laterali in piedi.'

Oswald von Wolkenstein Ritt

Italy

● Italy. The Ride (Ritt) of Oswald von Wolkenstein, named after the celebrated mediaeval troubadour who lived here, is an event with games on horseback. It is held every June on the Sciliar Plateau.

Italy. A set course includes games and
tournaments that require ability, speed
and precision.

Italy. Rider and horse must work in perfect harmony to be able to deal with the narrow spaces of each obstacle.

Puzta
horsemen
Hungary

from 666 to 669 ●
Hungary. During the
equestrian events held on
the *puszta*, the *czikos* –
Magyar cowboys – show
off with daredevil and
dramatic acrobatics.

Ride of the Kings
Czech Republic

- Czech Republic. Once widespread throughout Moravia, today the Ride of the Kings is held only in the village of Vlcnov. During the festivities, which are part of the Easter celebrations, the horses' manes and coats are decorated with multicolor ribbons.

672-673 • Czech Republic. A triumph of colors accompanies the King, in the center, escorted by two horsemen.

673 • Czech Republic. Damsels dressed in the rich traditional costumes of Vlcnov participate in the Ride of the Kings.

Fantasia
Morocco

674 and 675 ● Morocco. Fantasia are ceremonial simulations of a cavalry charge, symbolized by the shots fired into the air.

from 676 to 679 ● Morocco. Fantasia is an opportunity to revive warrior traditions as well as a patriotic sense of belonging.

Durbar Festival
Nigeria

• Nigeria. The celebrations of the Durbar Festival start at the end of Ramadan. The parade features fast-paced riding, in which participants raise their lances and swords to the sky.

682-683 ● Nigeria. The dark faces of the men blend with the black coats of the horses, thereby emphasizing the colors of the garments.

683 ● Nigeria. Nigerian and Berber ponies, which are small, agile and docile horses, play a starring role in the Durbar Festival.

Buskashi

Afghanistan

684 and 685 ● Afghanistan. The *Buskashi* is the Afghan national sport; it is a horseback struggle to win the body of a decapitated goat.

686-687 ● Afghanistan. The *Buskashi* is not really a team game. The aim is simply to better everybody else.

Afghanistan. Violence plays a central role in trying to get possession of the goat's carcass, or what remains of it at the end of the contest.

Litang
Festival
China

from 690 to 693 •
China. Each year on
Litang plateau in Tibet,
thousands of people
meet to challenge one
another in tests of skill on
horseback.

● China. The participants in the
Litang festival are from a tribe that
was once composed of ferocious
warriors. Today this legacy is
manifested in a spectacular
festival.

Omak Stampede
USA

696 ● USA. A calf is immobilized with
a halter during the Omak Stampede.

696-697 ● USA. A cowboy throws
the lasso.

Rodeo
USA

698 • USA. A competitor in the Cowtown Rodeo, held in New Jersey, throws himself on a bull to wrestle it to the ground.

698-699 • USA. Having roped its horns, two cowboys win control of a young bull.

USA. A participant at the Buffalo Bill Cody Stampede Fourth of July Rodeo follows a bull on horseback.

● USA. The rodeo calls for great physical effort by horses and their riders.

Rodeo
Canada

Canada.
As shown by the cowboy's
face, wrestling with a
young bull demands great
physical effort.

706 and 706-707 ● USA. The rodeo is not without a violent aspect, as by the calf's desperate flight from the mounted cowboy.

708-709 ● USA. A cowboy enters the ring.

USA. A cowboy can barely control this bucking horse in a bronco saddle-riding competition, which consists of riding a saddled foal, or bronco.

USA. During a contest, two team members attempt to control a wild horse.

714 and 715 • USA. Remaining on a wild horse is a test that requires the utmost strength.

716-717 • Canada. Dramatic falls are an attraction for the crowd at a rodeo.

VISIT THE HISTORIC
ROCKYVIEW HOTEL
STEAKHOUSE DANCEHALL

Rodeo

Australia

Australia. Breakaways, falls, and roll-overs are always a wild-card threat at rodeos.

Australia. The powerful ringers are accustomed to falling, but the same thing cannot be said of the untamed horses participating in rodeos. In fact, the horses are the ones that usually get hurt.

Rodeo de la Semana Criolla
Uruguay

Uruguay. During Creole week in Montevideo, Argentine, Brazilian and Uruguyuan *gauchos* challenge one another in various rodeos.

● Uruguay. Horses and *gauchos* offer acrobatic displays.

AUTHORS Biographies

▪ **GABRIELE BOISELLE**

Gabriele Boiselle, who has worked professionally for many years, is one of the world's most famous equestrian photographer and her work is regularly presented in the most important horse-racing periodicals. She has also published a number of successful books.

▪ **HENRY DALLAL**

Henry Dallal, who was born in Iran, is a landscape and nature photographer. His work has appeared in such publications as The Los Angeles Times, Hermes, Country Life, The Daily Telegraph, Household Cavalry Journal and Climbing. His books include *Pageantry and Performance: The Household Cavalry in a Celebration of Pictures*, the outcome of six years of work dedicated to following the Household Cavalry of Britain's Royal Guard. The results of this project have been exhibited at Windsor Castle, Kensington Palace, and the Royal Geographical Society. Dallal was also appointed to photograph H.R.H Queen Elizabeth for the cover of *All the Queen's Horses*, a tribute to Her Majesty's Jubilee. He has also contributed to *Horse Gunners: A Photographic Record of The King's Troop of the Royal Horse Artillery.*

▪ **ATTILA KORBELY**

Attila Korbely is a nature photographer that has been taking pictures since his childhood. He has worked for the most important photo magazines, and published extensively on photography and ecology, becoming the most published nature photographer in Hungary. He has served as an equipment tester for Canon, as chief nature photographer for Hungary's National Geographic Magazine, and is currently president of Nimrod: The Hungarian Nature Photographers Society. Mr. Korbely has undertaken more than 10 photo expeditions in search of stories on musk oxen, deer, etc., and on the world's most endangered areas. He has spent many weeks from season to season with the Takhi horses on the Hungarian *puszta* and in the Pentezug Bioreservation, recording them from birth to death, playing, fighting, feeding, and breeding.

PAOLO MANILI

Paolo Manili was born in Milan in 1949. A professional journalist, horse expert and a member of the International Alliance of Equestrian Journalists, he was for many years an editor with Cavallo Magazine and Lo Sperone, and continues to contribute to these specialized monthlies. For ten years he wrote the equestrian and riding column for several leading Italian dailies (Il Resto del Carlino, La Nazione and Il Giorno). From 1976 to the present he has reported on the world's major equestrian events. Manili has also headed the press office for international show jumping events, including several World Cup qualifiers in Bologna and also the Milan Masters. He has collaborated with periodicals such as Capital, Gente Viaggi and Polo International. For years he handled the series of manuals for Edizioni Equestri, including Guida del Cavaliere. He also wrote the book *Graziano Mancinelli – La leggenda di un cavaliere* (Poligrafici Editoriale).

SENIO SENSI

Senio Sensi was born in Siena in 1941. As a journalist, he has collaborated with periodicals and television stations in Siena and outside the city. For eight years he was Governor of the Noble Contrada of the Goose and is currently Managing Director of the Consortium for the Protection of the Palio, in charge of Communications and Image for the Siena festival. He is co-founder and director of the magazine Il Carroccio di Siena, which discusses the city's history, culture and events.

MEDFORD TAYLOR

Medford Taylor was born in Conway, North Carolina. His passion for horses has been the hallmark of his thirty-year career. As a freelance photographer, he has worked for numerous international periodicals, including GEO, Newsweek, TIME and National Geographic Magazine. Taylor has won a number of prizes, notably awards from the Virginia News Photographers Association and the White House News Photographers Association, and he participated in international photo exhibitions, including the 1997 Visa Pour L'Image international photo festival in Perpignan, France.

INDEX

PHOTO CREDITS

Page 145 M. Watson/Ardea
Pages 146-147 Alamy Images
Pages 148-149 Alamy Images
Pages 150-151 Alamy Images
Page 152 Alamy Images
Page 153 Alamy Images
Page 154-155 Kit Houghton/Corbis/Contrasto
Pages 156-157 Mark Barrett
Page 158 Gabriele Boiselle/Archiv Boiselle
Pages 158-159 Gabriele Boiselle/Archiv Boiselle
Pages 160-161 Gabriele Boiselle/Archiv Boiselle
Pages 162-163 Gabriele Boiselle/Archiv Boiselle
Pages 164-165 Gabriele Boiselle/Archiv Boiselle
Pages 166-167 Attila Korbely
Pages 168-169 Galen Rowell/Corbis/Contrasto
Pages 170-171 Gabriele Boiselle/Archiv Boiselle
Pages 172-173 David Stoecklein/Corbis/Contrasto
Pages 174-175 Mark Barrett
Pages 176-177 Mark Barrett
Pages 178-179 Mark Barrett
Pages 180-181 Jeff Vanuga/Corbis/Contrasto
Pages 182-183 Stuart Westmorland/Corbis/Contrasto
Page 185 Mark Barrett
Page 189 Gabriele Boiselle/Archiv Boiselle
Pages 190-191 H. Kuczka/Blickwinkel
Page 191 Mark Barrett
Page 192 Alamy Images
Page 193 Alamy Images
Pages 194-195 Marion and Hans Kuczka
Page 196 Attila Korbely

Page 197 Vincent Munier
Pages 198-199 Marion and Hans Kuczka
Page 199 Gabriele Boiselle/Archiv Boiselle
Pages 200-201 Gabriele Boiselle/Archiv Boiselle
Page 201 Gabriele Boiselle/Archiv Boiselle
Pages 202-203 Marielle Andresson/Archiv Boiselle
Pages 204-205 Mark Barrett
Page 206 Mark Barrett
Pages 206-207 Mark Barrett
Page 208 Marion and Hans Kuczka
Page 209 L. Lenz/Blickwinkel
Pages 210-211 Layne Kennedy/Corbis/Contrasto
Page 212 Darrell Gulin/Corbis/Contrasto
Page 213 Darrell Gulin/Corbis/Contrasto
Page 214 Kit Houghton/Corbis/Contrasto
Page 215 Kit Houghton/Corbis/Contrasto
Pages 216-217 Gabriele Boiselle/Archiv Boiselle
Page 218 Gabriele Boiselle/Archiv Boiselle
Page 219 Marion and Hans Kuczka
Page 220 Gabriele Boiselle/Archiv Boiselle
Page 221 Gabriele Boiselle/Archiv Boiselle
Page 222 Mark Barrett
Pages 223 Mark Barrett
Pages 224-225 Gabriele Boiselle/Archiv Boiselle
Pages 226-227 Mark Barrett
Page 227 Mark Barrett
Page 228 Mark Barrett
Page 229 Gabriele Boiselle/Archiv Boiselle
Page 230 Mark Barrett
Page 231 Attila Korbely
Page 232 Gabriele Boiselle/Archiv Boiselle
Page 233 Mark Barrett
Page 234 Gabriele Boiselle/Archiv Boiselle
Page 235 Mark Barrett
Page 236 Gabriele Boiselle/Archiv Boiselle

Page 237 Alejandro Diaz Diez/Agefotostock/Marka
Pages 238-239 Gabriele Boiselle/Archiv Boiselle
Pages 240-241 Mark Barrett
Pages 242-243 Mark Barrett
Page 244 L. Lenz/Blickwinkel
Page 245 L. Lenz/Blickwinkel
Page 246 Alamy Images
Page 247 Alamy Images
Page 248 Alamy Images
Page 249 Alamy Images
Page 251 Gabriele Boiselle/Archiv Boiselle
Page 253 Gabriele Boiselle/Archiv Boiselle
Page 257 L. Lenz/Blickwinkel
Page 258 Gabriele Boiselle/Archiv Boiselle
Pages 258-259 Gabriele Boiselle/Archiv Boiselle
Pages 260-261 Gabriele Boiselle/Archiv Boiselle
Pages 262-263 Gabriele Boiselle/Archiv Boiselle
Page 264 Danegger/Agefotostock/Marka
Page 265 Wittek/Agefotostock/Marka
Page 266 Gabriele Boiselle/Archiv Boiselle
Page 267 Marielle Andersson/Archiv Boiselle
Page 268 Soumagne/Agefotostock/Marka
Page 269 Gabriele Boiselle/Archiv Boiselle
Page 270 L. Lenz/Blickwinkel
Page 271 Gabriele Boiselle/Archiv Boiselle
Page 272 Mark Barrett
Pages 272-273 Mark Barrett
Page 274 Ch. Slawik/Edition Boiselle
Page 275 L. Lenz/Blickwinkel
Pages 276-277 Georgie Holland/Agefotostock/Contrasto
Pages 278-279 Gabriele Boiselle/Archiv Boiselle

PHOTO CREDITS

Pages 396-397 Medford Taylor
Pages 398-399 Medford Taylor
Page 401 Tiziana and Gianni Baldizzone/ Corbis/Contrasto
Page 405 David Stoecklein/Corbis/ Contrasto
Pages 406-407 Alamy Images
Page 408 David Stoecklein/Corbis/ Contrasto
Page 409 David Stoecklein/Corbis/ Contrasto
Pages 410-411 Tony Arruza/Corbis/ Contrasto
Page 412 Ariel Skelley/Corbis/Contrasto
Pages 412-413 Ariel Skelley/Corbis/Contrasto
Pages 414-415 L. Lenz/Blickwinkel
Page 415 L. Lenz/Blickwinkel
Page 416 David Stoecklein/Corbis/ Contrasto
Page 417 Gabriele Boiselle/Archiv Boiselle
Pages 418-419 Mark Barrett
Pages 420-421 Gabriele Boiselle/Archiv Boiselle
Page 422 Kit Houghton/Corbis/Contrasto
Page 423 Kit Houghton/Corbis/Contrasto
Page 424 G.Lacz/Panda Photo
Pages 424-425 Kit Houghton/Corbis/ Contrasto
Page 426 Kit Houghton/Corbis/Contrasto
Pages 426-427 Mark Barrett
Page 428 Setboun/Corbis/Contrasto
Page 429 Setboun/Corbis/Contrasto
Pages 430-431 M. Rutkiewicz/Blickwinkel
Page 433 Henry Dallal
Page 439 Eligio Paoni/Contrasto
Pages 440-441 Henry Dallal
Page 441 Henry Dallal
Page 442 Benoit Decout/Rea/Contrasto
Pages 442-443 Tim Graham/Corbis/ Contrasto

Page 444 Henry Dallal
Page 445 Henry Dallal
Page 446 Tim Graham/Corbis/Contrasto
Pages 446-447 Jeremy Horner/Corbis/ Contrasto
Pages 448-449 Henry Dallal
Page 449 Henry Dallal
Pages 450-451 Eligio Paoni/Contrasto
Page 452 Eligio Paoni/Contrasto
Page 453 Eligio Paoni/Contrasto
Pages 454-455 Eligio Paoni/Contrasto
Pages 456-457 Marco Pesaresi/Contrasto
Pages 458-459 Mal Langsdon/Reuters/ Contrasto
Page 460 Alamy Images
Page 461 Alamy Images
Page 462 Jeff Greenberg/Lonely Planet Images
Pages 462-463 Marka
Page 464 Macduff Everton/Corbis/Contrasto
Pages 464-465 Macduff Everton/Corbis/ Contrasto
Pages 466 Paul A. Souders/Corbis/ Contrasto
Page 467 Richard Cummins/Corbis/ Contrasto
Page 468 Richard Hamilton Smith/Corbis/ Contrasto
Pages 468-469 Tim Thompson/Corbis/ Contrasto
Page 470 Andres Blomqvist/Lonely Planet Images
Pages 470-471 Yann Arthus-Bertrand/ Corbis/Contrasto
Pages 472-473 Yann Arthus-Bertrand/ Corbis/Contrasto
Page 473 Yann Arthus-Bertrand/ Corbis/Contrasto
Pages 474-475 Yann Arthus-Bertrand/ Corbis/Contrasto

Page 477 Mark Barrett
Page 479 Jacques Toffi /Archiv Boiselle
Page 483 Gabriele Boiselle/Archiv Boiselle
Page 484 Kit Houghton/Corbis/Contrasto
Page 485 Kit Houghton/Corbis/Contrasto
Pages 486-487 Lorraine O'Sullivan/Inpho
Page 488 Gabriele Boiselle/Archiv Boiselle
Page 489 Jacques Toffi/Archiv Boiselle
Pages 490-491 Gabriele Boiselle/Archiv Boiselle
Pages 492-493 Kit Houghton/Corbis/ Contrasto
Pages 494-495 Allsport/Inpho
Page 496 Gabriele Boiselle/Archiv Boiselle
Pages 496-497 Gabriele Boiselle/Archiv Boiselle
Page 498 Kit Houghton/Corbis/Contrasto
Page 499 Gabriele Boiselle/Archiv Boiselle
Pages 500-501 Jim Hllander/Reuters/ Contrasto
Page 502 Mark Barrett
Pages 502-503 Mark Barrett
Page 504 Toni Anzenberger/ Anzenberger/Contrasto
Page 505 Toni Anzenberger/ Anzenberger/Contrasto
Pages 506-507 Toni Anzenberger/ Anzenberger/Contrasto
Page 507 Toni Anzenberger/ Anzenberger/Contrasto
Page 508 Michael Crabtree/Reuters/ Contrasto
Page 509 Michael Crabtree/Reuters/ Contrasto
Pages 510-511 Ralph A. Clevenger/ Corbis/Contrasto
Pages 512-513 Mark Barrett
Pages 514-515 Paul A. Souders/Corbis/ Contrasto
Pages 516-517 Mark Barrett

733

PHOTO CREDITS

Page 518 Gabriele Boiselle/Archiv Boiselle

Page 519 Marielle Andresson/Archiv Boiselle

Pages 520-521 Gabriele Boiselle/Archiv Boiselle

Page 521 Allsport/Inpho

Page 522 Jacques Toffi /Archiv Boiselle

Page 523 Gabriele Boiselle/Archiv Boiselle

Pages 524-525 Kit Houghton/Corbis/Contrasto

Page 526 Gabriele Boiselle/Archiv Boiselle

Page 527 Michael Crabtree/Reuters/Contrasto

Pages 528-529 Mark Barrett

Pages 530-531 Jonathan Blair/Corbis/Contrasto

Page 531 Jonathan Blair/Corbis/Contrasto

Pages 532-533 Mark Barrett

Pages 534-535 Pierre Vauthey/Corbis Sygma/Contrasto

Pages 536-537 Specht/Laif/Contrasto

Pages 538-539 Kevin Fleaming/Corbis/Contrasto

Pages 540-541 Kelly-Mooney Photography/Corbis/Contrasto

Pages 542-543 Gabriele Boiselle/Archiv Boiselle

Pages 544-545 John Walton/Empics/Contrasto

Pages 546-547 Morgan Treacy/Inpho

Pages 548-549 Patrick Bolger/Inpho

Pages 550-551 Inpho

Page 551 Lorraine O'Sullivan/Inpho

Pages 552-553 Ruben Sprich/Reuters/Contrasto

Pages 554-555 Gabriele Boiselle/Archiv Boiselle

Page 556 Mark Barrett

Page 557 Ray Stubblebine/Reuters/Contrasto

Pages 558-559 Skip Dickstein/Corbis/Contrasto

Pages 560-561 John Sommers/Reuters/Contrasto

Pages 562-563 Rick Rickman/NewSport/Corbis/Contrasto

Pages 564-565 Marcelo Del Pozo/Reuters/Contrasto

Pages 566-567 Bobby Yip/Reuters/Contrasto

Page 568 John Walton/Empics/Contrasto

Page 569 Jack Atley/Reuters/Contrasto

Pages 570-571 Mark Barrett

Page 572 Morgan Treacy/Inpho

Pages 572-573 Jack Atley/Reuters/Contrasto

Pages 574-575 Mark Barrett

Pages 576-577 Kevin R. Morris/Corbis/Contrasto

Page 578 Darren Staples/Reuters/Contrasto

Page 579 Mike Cassese/Reuters/Contrasto

Page 581 Benali-Dufour/Gamma/Contrasto

Page 583 Manfred Horvarth/Anzenberger/Contrasto

Page 587 Jacques Toffi/Archiv Boiselle

Page 588 left, center and right Gabriele Boiselle/Archiv Boiselle

Page 589 Gabriele Boiselle/Archiv Boiselle

Pages 590-591 Mark Barrett

Pages 592-593 Mark Barrett

Page 594 J.D. Dallet/Agefotostock/Marka

Pages 594-595 Corbis/Contrasto

Page 596 Nik Wheeler/Corbis/Contrasto

Page 597 Mark Barrett

Page 598 Gabriele Boiselle/Archiv Boiselle

Page 599 Gabriele Boiselle/Archiv Boiselle

Pages 600-601 Benali-Dufour/Gamma/Contrasto

Page 602 Benali-Dufour/Gamma/Contrasto

Page 603 Remi Benali/Gamma/Contrasto

Pages 604-605 Benali-Dufour/Gamma/Contrasto

Page 606 Manfred Horvarth/Anzenberger/Contrasto

Page 607 Manfred Horvarth/Anzenberger/Contrasto

Pages 608-609 Jerry Cooke/Corbis/Contrasto

Pages 610-611 Alamy Images

Page 613 Alamy Images

Page 615 Marcello Bertinetti/Archivio White Star

Page 621 Baci/Corbis/Contrasto

Page 622 Huber/Laif/Contrasto

Pages 622-623 Huber/Laif/Contrasto

Page 624 Huber/Laif/Contrasto

Page 625 Gabriele Boiselle/Archiv Boiselle

Page 626 Antonio Attini/Archivio White Star

Page 627 Antonio Attini/Archivio White Star

Page 628 Antonio Attini/Archivio White Star

Page 629 Antonio Attini/Archivio White Star

Pages 630-631 Antonio Attini/Archivio White Star

Page 632 Gabriele Boiselle/Archiv Boiselle

Page 633 Gabriele Boiselle/Archiv Boiselle

Pages 634-635 Gabriele Boiselle/Archiv Boiselle

Pages 636-637 Gabriele Boiselle/Archiv Boiselle

Pages 638 Dani Cardona/Reuters/Contrasto

Page 639 Bialobrzeski/Laif/Contrasto

Pages 640-641 Dani Cardona/Reuters/Contrasto

Page 641 Abbie Enock; Travel Ink/Corbis/Contrasto

Page 642 and 643 Huber/Laif/Contrasto

France. Big eyes, graceful features and a prominent forehead are distinctive of the magnificent Arabian horse.